The Kitchen Sessions

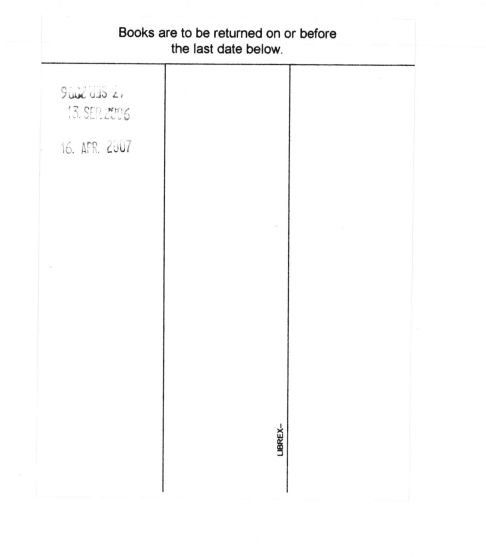

THE KITCHEN SESSIONS
WITH CHARLIE TROTTER

Recipes by Charlie Trotter

Photography by Tim Turner, *Wine Notes by* Brian Cronin

Illustrations by Matthias Merges and Mitchell Rice

 Ten Speed Press, Berkeley, California

CONTENTS

FOREWORD

What a joy to experience many great dishes
in the course of an evening,
each one new, exciting and beautifully presented.

Ah, the joys of eating. Food and wine is such a pleasure...and as you have chosen
to read this book, you most likely agree.

In The Kitchen Sessions, Charlie Trotter brings us his perspective on food and
wine and relates it to the creation of great improvisational music. As in any creative
endeavor, the end result is a direct reflection of the philosophy of the artist.
In Charlie's case, his relating to the great jazz masters of our time makes perfect
sense—cause this man can jam.

Charlie is all about spontaneity. So much so, that you may find it interesting to
know that the dishes included in this book were created with no advance planning
or script. They were developed as he filmed the companion television cooking
show. Charlie began each segment with nothing more formal than thoughts about
a particular type of dish or combination of flavors and ingredients assembled to
'play with'. Only after the show were the recipes written to support the dishes that
were created on the set. This is the Trotter way. The result is fresh and alive,
and you never know quite what to expect. For me this is what cooking is all about.

Charlie also practices this philosophy in his restaurant. Having enjoyed well over 100 meals at Trotter's in Chicago, I have never been served the same dish twice. What would be the point? What a joy to experience many great dishes in the course of an evening, each one new, exciting, and beautifully presented. And there is no doubt in my mind that Charlie and other great chefs find as much joy in creating these great meals as we get from experiencing them. Their cooking is very personal, and instantly develops a relationship with the diner. I am reminded of the great meals I have had that were created by the amazing chefs Fredy Girardet in Switzerland and Tetsuya Wakuda in Australia, who epitomize the concept of cooking from the heart, not as a technician.

This book captures Charlie's spirit and enthusiasm. There are no rules. Try different things—don't be intimidated—allow yourself to think, adapt, and explore. A professional kitchen and staff are not required. In your kitchen, you are the master chef; you create your own music.

STEVEN GREYSTONE—International Food and Wine Connoisseur

The food I create really evolves from one simple question:

what do I like to eat?

I don't believe that there is a perfect cuisine.
Cooking is a form of expression
that combines ideas about cooking and eating
in a way that a lot of people, from the home cook
to professional chefs, can understand.

I am greatly inspired by the great jazz musicians of the '40s, '50s, and '60s who routinely went into a studio or club and played live sets. The resulting "sessions" would represent a given moment. Miles Davis may have played "Stella by Starlight" or "My Funny Valentine" hundreds of times, but he played them differently in each session. Cooking is exactly like playing music, and once historical precedence and classical ideas are understood, the possibilities are only as limited as the artist's imagination. It's about understanding classic combinations from western Europe and Asia and paying respect to those ideals. It's about approaching cooking with the same spontaneity that defines a jazz session—hence the name *The Kitchen Sessions.*

Cooking is really not that difficult. In fact, it's more about love and touch and caring than about special techniques or magical recipes. It is about caring for and loving the foodstuffs you're working with and caring for and loving the people you are cooking for. Preparing great-tasting, nutritious food merely stems from the desire that is present in each of us to do something truly special for family, friends, and

Cooking is like
music

The
is among the most
that we

art of cooking
intimate things
can do for another.

even those we may not yet be acquainted with. For the art of cooking, that is the act of gathering foodstuffs, preparing them, and serving them, is among the most intimate things that we can do for another. Indeed, since every sense—touching, smelling, seeing, tasting, and hearing—is engaged, at times even profoundly, the entire process more often than not verges on the sensual. And when food and wine stimulate and excite the palate, which in turn stimulates the mind, the act of eating becomes so much more than that of attaining sustenance. It is more about achieving a higher good intellectually, spiritually, and sensually.

The greatest joy in all of cooking though is to understand and appreciate the extraordinary spontaneity inherent in the process. Foodstuffs can be interchanged at will depending on what is available, and what you feel like eating or serving. You can use chicken instead of beef, or salmon instead of chicken, or shrimp instead of salmon, or you can omit the fish or meat altogether. Rice can be used in lieu of pasta, or legumes in place of rice. Any degree of acid can be added through the use of citrus or vinegar, or any intensity of heat through the use of chiles. Practically any type of herb can be used in a dish depending on your preferences. Some like strong, fruity olive oil. Some prefer mild, vaguely fragrant olive oil. One time you might make a fruit tart with peaches, the next time with plums or apples.

This time you might serve it with vanilla-tarragon ice cream, next time with a
curried yogurt sorbet. Today you may prefer to grill your fish, tomorrow to steam
it. Almonds, goat cheese, and dried currants can be used in the endive salad this
time and replaced with hazelnuts, Maytag blue cheese, and sultanas the next.
You get the idea. In *The Kitchen Sessions* my intention is to emphasize the notion
of interchangeability and the addition or subtraction of foodstuffs in order to best
achieve results that will suit your desires. The recipes here, as should always
be the case, are meant to be used as guides or as inspiration. And the best way
to be a successful cook is to really love to eat. If you truly love eating and tasting
and smelling, you will eventually arrive at a most satisfactory result.

There is, however, a historical precedent to considering flavors and textures that
cannot be completely ignored. So, studying recipes and the frequent exercise of
cooking will help you progress to the point at which you can improvise and be
spontaneous with flavors and textures, as well as personal preferences. The key to
everything though is to enjoy yourself. Eating is the one great sensual pleasure that
we all enjoy several times a day. So go ahead and have fun with the entire process
of obtaining the foodstuffs, preparing and cooking them, and serving them forth.

key to everything is
yourself

Chapter

1

Soup

PUMPKIN SOUP WITH PHEASANT BREAST AND FRIED GINGER

The simple flavors of this soup produce extraordinary elegance. Ginger and dried cranberries accentuate the sweetness of the pumpkin and make the soup nearly pop with flavor, while at the same time they counter the lusciousness of the pheasant. Crispy pepitos add a playfulness that could also be achieved by adding toasted almond or hazelnut pieces. Butternut, acorn, or blue hubbard squash could easily be substituted for the pumpkin, and lobster works nicely in place of the pheasant.

SERVES 4

1 small pumpkin (about 1½ pounds), halved and seeded

Salt and pepper

3 tablespoons olive oil

12 sprigs thyme

¼ cup Preserved Ginger (see page 211)

2 cups Chicken Stock (see page 201)

3 tablespoons butter

½ cup julienned fresh ginger

½ cup plus 1 tablespoon canola oil

2 pheasant breasts, skin on

¼ cup dried cranberries, chopped and rehydrated

¼ cup pepitos (green pumpkin seeds)

4 teaspoons pumpkin seed oil

METHOD—To prepare the pumpkin: Rub the pumpkin with the olive oil and season with salt and pepper. Place the pumpkin halves upside down on a sheet pan and place 8 of the thyme sprigs under the pumpkins. Add ¼ inch of water and roast at 350 degrees for 45 to 60 minutes, or until the pumpkins are tender.

To prepare the soup: Purée the Preserved Ginger and any ginger syrup, the stock, and the pulp from the cooked pumpkin until smooth, and season to taste with salt and pepper. Cook the mixture over medium heat for 5 minutes, or until warm. Whisk in the butter and season to taste with salt and pepper.

To prepare the ginger: Place the julienned ginger and ½ cup of room temperature canola oil in a small saucepan. Warm the oil over medium heat and cook for 8 to 10 minutes, or until golden brown and crispy. Drain on paper towels.

To prepare the pheasant: Season the pheasant with salt and pepper. Add the remaining 1 tablespoon canola oil to a hot sauté pan over medium heat. Add the pheasant and cook for 3 to 5 minutes on each side, or until just cooked. Let rest for 3 minutes and then thinly slice. Season to taste with salt and pepper.

ASSEMBLY—Ladle the soup into 4 shallow bowls. Arrange the pheasant slices in the center and sprinkle the dried cranberries, pepitos, fried ginger, and the remaining thyme leaves around the bowl. Top with freshly ground black pepper and drizzle the pumpkin seed oil around the soup.

WINE NOTES—A full-bodied, lean Puligny-Montrachet from Domaine Leflaive or Jean Marc Boillot would be a good match with this soup. Their acidity balances the sweetness of the soup, while the oak makes the pumpkin seeds jump out.

COLD CUCUMBER AND YOGURT SOUP
WITH OYSTERS AND CAVIAR

This dish is especially refreshing on a warm summer day.

It goes together very quickly because there is

no cooking involved;

the cucumbers, yogurt, and a little lemon juice are merely blended together.

Shrimp or salmon can be added for a more lavish presentation or to provide more substance.

For a wonderful vegetarian first course, omit the oysters

and add a couple of additional vegetables.

SERVES 4

2 English cucumbers,
peeled and chopped

1 cup plain yogurt

3 tablespoons freshly squeezed
lemon juice

Salt and pepper

1 small yellow tomato, peeled,
seeded and diced

1 tablespoon olive oil

1 cup Hot and Sour Cucumbers
(see page 207)

16 small oysters, shucked

5 tablespoons plus 1 teaspoon caviar

2 tablespoons radish sprouts

2 teaspoons dill sprigs

4 teaspoons Dill Oil (see page 203)

METHOD—To prepare the soup: Purée the cucumbers, yogurt, and lemon juice until smooth and season to taste with salt and pepper. Refrigerate until ready to use.

To prepare the tomato: Toss the diced tomato with the olive oil and season to taste with salt and pepper.

ASSEMBLY—Stir the soup and ladle into 4 shallow bowls. Place some of the diced tomato in the center of each bowl and arrange some of the Hot and Sour Cucumbers at 4 points around the tomatoes. Place an oyster on each mound of cucumbers and top each oyster with 1 teaspoon of the caviar. Sprinkle a few of the radish sprouts around the bowls. Sprinkle the dill sprigs on the soup and drizzle the Dill Oil around the bowls. Top with freshly ground black pepper.

WINE NOTES—This refreshing soup requires an equally refreshing wine. The key to finding the right wine for this dish is matching the oysters and caviar, and the crisp acidity and mineral flavors of a Chablis are perfect. Either the Moreau Chablis "Vaillons" or a Sancerre by Lucien Crochet would do the trick.

ROASTED GARLIC—WHITE BEAN SOUP WITH WHITE BEAN—PROSCIUTTO GALETTES

White bean soup is so simple, yet so profound.

The beans are cooked until they barely maintain their texture, and the resulting flavor is redolent of

the vegetables and garlic they are cooked with. A small white bean galette adds texture and substance,

which helps push this sensual soup over the top.

Tomato concassé could be added to provide a pleasant acidic note. For the

ultimate in richness and luxury,

serve a piece of seared foie gras in the center of each bowl.

SERVES 4

3 bulbs garlic, cloves separated and peeled

4 cups Chicken Stock (see page 201)

4 cups cooked white beans (such as cannellini or navy beans)

2 tablespoons chopped fresh parsley leaves

Salt and pepper

½ pound thinly sliced prosciutto, fat trimmed, meat julienned

2 tablespoons butter

METHOD—To prepare the garlic: Simmer the garlic in the stock for 45 minutes, or until soft. Drain the garlic, reserving the stock and the garlic separately.

To prepare the beans: Purée the white beans with three quarters of the garlic until smooth. Place 1 cup of the purée in a small bowl and fold in the parsley. Season to taste with salt and pepper and refrigerate for 1 hour.

To prepare the soup: Add the reserved cooking liquid to the remaining white bean purée and blend until fully incorporated. Return the soup to a saucepan and warm over medium heat. Season to taste with salt and pepper.

To prepare the galettes: Fold one-third of the prosciutto into the chilled white bean purée. Fill four 2-inch-diameter by 1-inch-high molds with the bean purée. Place the butter in a hot sauté pan over medium heat and add the molds. Cook for 2 minutes, or until the bottoms are golden brown. Turn the molds, cook for 1 minute on the other side, and carefully remove the molds from the cakes. Cook for 2 more minutes, or until the cakes are golden brown.

ASSEMBLY—Place some of the proscuitto in the center of each shallow bowl and top with a galette. Mound the remaining proscuitto on top of the galettes. Carefully ladle the soup into the bowls. Sprinkle the remaining garlic cloves around the bowls and top with freshly ground black pepper.

WINE NOTES—The smokiness of a white Burgundy from Chassagne-Montrachet will balance perfectly with the rich, sweet, earthiness of white beans, but still allow the sweet flavor of the roasted garlic to shine through. Ramonet or Colin-Deleger both produce wines that will blend seamlessly with this dish.

SWEET CORN SOUP WITH SHRIMP
AND SHELLFISH OIL

The combination of corn and shellfish is truly special,

with the natural sweetness of the corn perfectly accentuating the

rich flavor of the shellfish.

This soup is simple to make

and it is very versatile—it can be presented either in a rustic or more upscale manner.

Chicken or duck can be substituted for the shrimp

with fine results, or a couple of chiles can be sautéed with the onion,

if a spicier soup is desired.

SERVES 4

3 cups corn kernels

1 cup small-diced onions

3 tablespoons butter

4 cups Chicken or Vegetable Stock
(see page 201, 220)

Salt and pepper

8 scallions, cut into 2-inch pieces

8 large shrimp, peeled and deveined

2 tablespoons canola oil

1 cup peeled, seeded,
and diced tomatoes

4 tablespoons Shellfish Oil
(see page 216)

METHOD—To prepare the soup: Sweat the corn and onions in 2 tablespoons butter for 10 minutes, or until the onions are translucent. Add 1 cup of the stock and cook for 10 minutes. Remove 1 cup of the corn mixture and set aside. Purée the remaining corn mixture and 2 cups stock until smooth and pass through a fine-mesh sieve. Cook the soup over medium heat for 5 minutes, or until warm, and season to taste with salt and pepper.

To prepare the scallions: Simmer the scallions in a small saucepan with the remaining 1 tablespoon of the butter and 1 cup of the stock for 5 to 7 minutes, or until the scallions are tender.

To prepare the shrimp: Season the shrimp with salt and pepper. Place the canola oil in a hot sauté pan, quickly add the shrimp, and cook for 3 minutes, or until just cooked. Add the tomatoes, and cook for 1 minute, or until the tomatoes are warm. Season to taste with salt and pepper.

ASSEMBLY—Place some of the reserved corn mixture and some of the braised scallions in the center of each bowl. Ladle the soup over the corn and top with 2 shrimp. Spoon some of the warm tomatoes around the bowls and drizzle with the Shellfish Oil. Top with freshly ground black pepper.

WINE NOTES—Viognier has always been a great wine to pair with shellfish, but to balance out the sweetness of the corn soup, try a crisper style from the U.S. Either La Jota from Howell Mountain or John Albans from Edna Valley will be a good match with this sweet, rich soup.

WILD MUSHROOM "CONSOMMÉ" WITH HERB BUTTER CROUTONS

This mushroom consommé is quite versatile, and it is surprisingly simple to make. It is both delicate and explosive in flavor, and although the croutons add some substance, the soup is incredibly light. If an earthier broth is desired, just reduce it more. To make this dish a full meal, add chunks of poached chicken and noodles or barley. For a special dinner, bite-sized mushroom or shrimp raviolis are a great addition.

SERVES 4

1 portobello mushroom, stemmed

1 cup shiitake mushrooms, stemmed

1 cup button mushrooms

2 sprigs rosemary

4 cloves garlic

½ cup water

Salt and pepper

¼ cup butter, melted

1 tablespoon chopped fresh chives

1 tablespoon chopped
fresh parsley leaves

1 teaspoon minced garlic

1 tablespoon minced shallot

8 ¼-inch-thick sourdough
baguette slices

Wild Mushroom Consommé
(see page 220)

2 tablespoons olive oil

METHOD—To prepare the mushrooms: Cut the portobello mushroom into quarters and place in an ovenproof pan with the shiitake mushrooms, button mushrooms, rosemary, garlic, and water. Season with salt and pepper and cover tightly. Roast at 350 degrees for 30 to 45 minutes, or until tender. Cut the roasted mushrooms into bite-sized pieces and season to taste with salt and pepper. Slice each garlic clove into 4 slices.

To prepare the croutons: Combine the butter, chives, parsley, minced garlic, and shallot in a small bowl and season to taste with salt and pepper. Place the sourdough slices on a sheet pan and brush with the butter mixture. Toast in the oven at 400 degrees for 12 to 15 minutes, or until light golden brown.

ASSEMBLY—Arrange some of the roasted mushrooms and garlic slices in the center of each bowl. Ladle some of the consommé into each bowl and drizzle the olive oil around the bowls. Top with freshly ground black pepper and place 2 croutons on top of the mushrooms.

WINE NOTES—The richness of mushrooms will usually push a dish into the red wine realm, but the delicate, aromatic qualities of this consommé make it perfectly suited to an earthy white wine. A Châteauneuf-du-Pape or Côte-du-Rhône blanc from producers such as Domaine de Vieux Telegraph or Beaucastel will mesh beautifully with this dish.

WARM ASPARAGUS SOUP WITH GOAT CHEESE—FILO PACKAGES AND BLACK OLIVES

This clean and elegant asparagus soup is a bit reserved, which makes it an intriguing dish. The goat cheese package adds crunchy and creamy textures, which provide an extravagant lushness, while the black olives bring everything into balance. Lightly pickled asparagus tips provide additional texture and whimsy and further emphasize the primary flavor of the dish. For a different twist, add sundried tomatoes, or even smoked chicken to the soup.

SERVES 4

1 cup julienned onions

1 tablespoon butter

Salt and pepper

3 sheets filo dough

¼ cup butter, melted

4 1½-ounce pieces goat cheese

16 asparagus spears, trimmed, blanched, and tips cut off and reserved

½ cup Pickling Juice (see page 211)

¼ cup olive oil

3 cups Vegetable Stock (see page 220)

1 teaspoon minced garlic

⅓ cup pitted and chopped oil-cured black olives

¼ cup chiffonade-cut fresh basil leaves

METHOD—To prepare the filo packages: Cook the onions in the butter over medium-high heat for 5 minutes, or until golden brown and caramelized. Season to taste with salt and pepper and let cool to room temperature.

Lay a piece of filo dough on a work surface and lightly brush with some of the melted butter. Cover with a second sheet of filo, brush again with the melted butter, cover with the remaining sheet of filo, and brush with melted butter. Cut the filo dough into four 4-to 5-inch squares. Spoon some of the caramelized onion in the center of each filo square and top with a piece of the goat cheese. Fold in 2 opposite corners of the filo, completely covering the goat cheese. Fold in the remaining 2 corners, creating a square. Place the filo packages on a parchment-lined sheet pan with the seams down, brush with melted butter, and refrigerate for 30 minutes. Remove the filo packages from the refrigerator and bake at 425 degrees for 20 minutes, or until golden brown.

To prepare the asparagus: Place the asparagus tips in the Pickling Juice and refrigerate for 30 minutes. Strain the Pickling Juice and reserve the asparagus tips. (The Pickling Juice may be refrigerated and reserved for another use.)

To prepare the asparagus soup: Purée the asparagus stems, olive oil, stock, and garlic until smooth. Pass the purée through a fine-mesh sieve and pour it into a saucepan. Cook over medium heat for 10 minutes, or until warm, and season to taste with salt and pepper.

ASSEMBLY—Place a mound of the pickled asparagus tips and black olives in the center of each bowl and top with a warm filo package. Carefully ladle the soup around the filo packages. Sprinkle the soup with the basil and top with freshly ground black pepper.

WINE NOTES—Asparagus can sometimes be difficult to pair with wine, but with the addition of goat cheese, a Loire Valley wine makes just the right pairing. A Savennierres by Domaine de Baumard or the Grand Cru Savennierres by Nicolas Joly "Clos de la Coulee de Serrant" would both be good choices.

filo package

asparagus tips

basil leaves

soup

Chapter

2

GRILLED BEEF TENDERLOIN COBB SALAD

This has to be one of my all-time favorite salads, because of the unrestrained variety of flavors and textures. Traditionally a cobb salad is made with chicken, but I use grilled beef because I prefer a little more substance.

I lay out the ingredients in the traditional manner, in rows on a bed of lettuce.

You can, of course, toss everything together and not bother with this special presentation.

The flavors and textures would certainly be the same, but sometimes the

striking composition

of a finished dish is reward enough for the extra trouble.

SERVES 4

1 shallot, minced

⅓ cup freshly squeezed lemon juice

2 tablespoons chopped fresh chives

1 cup olive oil

Salt and pepper

1⅓ cups peeled and diced red and yellow tomatoes

8 cups mesclun mix

8 slices proscuitto, juilienned

16 quail eggs, soft-boiled, peeled, and quartered

1⅓ cups diced avocado

8 ounces beef tenderloin, grilled, cooled, and diced

1⅓ cups crumbled blue cheese

12 grilled scallions, chilled and chopped

4 tablespoons 1-inch pieces chives

METHOD—To prepare the vinaigrette: Place the shallot, and lemon juice, in a small bowl. Slowly whisk in the olive oil, fold in the chopped chives, and season to taste with salt and pepper.

To prepare the tomatoes: Toss the diced tomatoes with 2 tablespoons of the vinaigrette and season to taste with salt and pepper.

To prepare the greens: Toss the mesclun mix with half of the vinaigrette and season to taste with salt and pepper.

ASSEMBLY—Arrange some of the mesclun greens to create a bed in the center of each plate. Arrange some of the proscuitto in a vertical line along the far left side of the greens. Next to the proscuitto, arrange some of the quail eggs, avocado, tomatoes, beef tenderloin, blue cheese, and scallions each in individual vertical lines to completely cover the mesclun mix. Top with freshly ground black pepper and sprinkle with the chive pieces. Drizzle the remaining vinaigrette over the salad.

WINE NOTES—This is a fun salad to eat and requires a fun wine. Strict flavor pairing is not always needed; sometimes eating and drinking for pure enjoyment is in order. Try a fruit forward style of Merlot like Robert Sinskey Vineyards or Cuvaison, both from the Napa Valley.

SALSIFY AND PICKLED SHIITAKE MUSHROOM SALAD WITH PORTOBELLO MUSHROOM VINAIGRETTE

This salad is very simple,

but its key ingredients have elegant and profound flavors:

the portobello mushrooms are earthy, the salsify sweet, the black walnuts rich,

the bacon pieces slightly salty, and the mâche buttery.

To literally and figuratively top them all off, a rich and tangy mushroom vinaigrette

is drizzled over and makes the dish really sing. For a variation try serving this salad warm

or placing a piece of chicken or beef right on top.

SERVES 4

4 stalks salsify

2 cups milk

1½ cups shiitake mushrooms, julienned

1 cup Pickling Juice (see page 211)

¾ cup cooked bacon pieces

1½ cups mâche

¼ cup black walnuts

Salt and pepper

Portobello Mushroom Vinaigrette (recipe follows)

1 tablespoon flat-leaf parsley chiffonade

½ teasoon sea salt

METHOD—To prepare the salsify: Peel the salsify, cut it into 3-inch pieces on the diagonal, and immediately place it in a saucepan and cover with the milk. Simmer for 10 minutes, or until the salsify is just tender. Remove the salsify from the milk and let cool. Cut each piece in half on the diagonal and then in half lengthwise.

To prepare the mushrooms: In a medium bowl, cover the mushrooms with the Pickling Juice and let marinate for 30 minutes. Drain the juice and set the mushrooms aside. (The Pickling Juice can be stored in the refrigerator and reserved for another use.)

peel salsify   cut diagonally into 3 inch pieces

To prepare the salad: Toss together the salsify, mushrooms, bacon, mâche, and walnuts and toss lightly with some of the vinaigrette. Season to taste with salt and pepper.

ASSEMBLY—Spoon a pool of the Portobello Mushroom Vinaigrette in the center of each plate. Arrange some of the salad in the center of the vinaigrette and top with the sea salt and freshly ground black pepper. Sprinkle the parsley over the salads.

WINE NOTES—The lingering smokiness of the bacon in this salad makes it a perfect match for a richer style Napa Valley Chardonnay or a white Burgundy. Puligny-Montrachet from Domaine Leflaive or a Vine Cliff Chardonnay both have enough toasty oak flavor to blend well with this dish.

Portobello Mushroom Vinaigrette

You can make this vinaigrette with any type of mushrooms.

YIELD: 1 CUP

1 grilled portobello mushroom, chopped

¼ cup balsamic vinegar

½ cup olive oil

Salt and pepper

METHOD—Purée the mushroom, balsamic vinegar, and olive oil until smooth and season to taste with salt and pepper.

SALAD OF BEETS, BELGIAN ENDIVE, GOAT CHEESE, AND ASIAN PEAR

This dish is quite simple to make, and although it doesn't seem like much, the flavors and textures are tremendously complex. Sweet, earthy beets; sharp, assertive Belgian endive; bitter, peppery radicchio; earthy, musty goat cheese; crunchy, meaty hazelnuts; and crisp, refreshing Asian pears merge into a seamless mélange of flavors. Each ingredient retains its characteristics, yet each contributes to the overall effect. For a more substantial dish, fan out slices of chicken or duck breast over the salad.

SERVES 4

8 baby red beets

8 baby yellow beets

2 tablespoons olive oil

Salt and pepper

1 shallot, minced

⅓ cup sherry wine vinegar

½ cup hazelnut oil

½ cup canola oil

1 small head Belgian endive, julienned

1 small head radicchio, shredded

1 large Asian pear, peeled, cored, and julienned

1 cup goat cheese, crumbled

¾ cup hazelnuts, toasted, skinned, and quartered

METHOD—To prepare the beets: Place the red and yellow beets in a saucepan and cover with water. Simmer for 15 to 20 minutes, or until tender. Shock the beets in ice water and remove the skin and stems. Slice the beets in half, toss with the olive oil, and season to taste with salt and pepper.

To prepare the vinaigrette: Place the shallot and sherry wine vinegar in a small bowl and slowly whisk in the hazelnut oil and canola oil. Season to taste with salt and pepper.

To prepare the salad: Toss the endive, radicchio, Asian pear, goat cheese, and hazelnuts with the vinaigrette and season to taste with salt and pepper.

ASSEMBLY—Place some of the salad in the center of each plate. Arrange the beets around the salad and top with freshly ground black pepper.

WINE NOTES—The beets add wonderful sweetness and earthy complexity to this dish. A dry style of Vouvray, such as Bourillon d'Orleans, is a wonderful balance to these characteristics, as well as being perfectly compatible with the goat cheese.

PRAWN AND HARICOTS VERTS SALAD WITH
ROASTED GARLIC—MUSTARD VINAIGRETTE

The secret to this dish is the vinaigrette.

The creamy roasted garlic is perfectly cut by the sharp mustard to make a sublime vinaigrette

that lightly coats the plump prawns, the crisp haricots verts, the luscious artichoke pieces,

and the cleansing sunchoke slices. Tarragon leaves lend the whole ensemble

a sweet perfume, and the drizzle of shellfish oil adds a delicate richness and flavor

that echoes the flavors of the prawns. This preparation is

a perfect prelude to roasted chicken

or grilled pork loin, or as the main course at lunch.

SERVES 4

8 steamed prawns, shelled, deveined, and halved lengthwise

4 cooked artichoke bottoms, cleaned and cut into wedges

20 haricots verts, blanched

2 tablespoons chopped fresh tarragon leaves

2 sunchokes, peeled and thinly sliced

Roasted Garlic–Mustard Vinaigrette (recipe follows)

Salt and pepper

½ cup snow pea sprouts

2 tablespoons plus 2 teaspoons Shellfish Oil (see page 216)

METHOD—To prepare the salad: Toss the prawns, artichoke bottoms, haricots verts, tarragon, and sunchokes with ½ cup of the Roasted Garlic–Mustard Vinaigrette and season to taste with salt and pepper.

ASSEMBLY—Place some of the salad in the center of each plate and sprinkle with the snow pea sprouts. Drizzle some of the Roasted Garlic–Mustard Vinaigrette and Shellfish Oil around the plate. Top with freshly ground black pepper.

WINE NOTES—Artichokes are the most difficult vegetable to pair with wine. They require a wine that is rich and earthy enough to neutralize the acidity of the artichokes without overpowering their sweetness. Loire Valley Chenin Blanc from Savennières has just the right earthy characteristics for the artichokes but doesn't hide the succulent flavor of the prawns.

Roasted Garlic—Mustard Vinaigrette

YIELD: 1⅓ CUPS

¼ cup Roasted Garlic Purée (see page 214)

1½ tablespoons Dijon mustard

¼ cup rice wine vinegar

¾ cup olive oil

Salt and pepper

METHOD—Purée the garlic, mustard, vinegar, and olive oil until smooth. Season to taste with salt and pepper.

INDIAN RED PEACH AND CRAB SALAD
WITH YOGURT–POPPYSEED DRESSING

The combination of luscious peach and sweet crabmeat is truly perfect—

each complements the other.

The nuances of the crab are further enhanced

by the flavors and textures of scallions, red bell pepper, and cucumbers.

A sweet, tart dressing of yogurt and orange juice drizzled over the peaches

and lettuce transforms this into a spirited salad; the poppyseeds and minced jalapeños provide

playful crunchiness and heat. This salad makes a splendid lunch,

or it can be served as an appetizer with dinner.

SERVES 4

¾ cup plain yogurt

1 tablespoon poppyseeds

1 jalapeño, seeded and minced

¼ cup freshly squeezed orange juice

½ cup freshly squeezed lime juice

Salt and pepper

1 cup fresh crabmeat

1½ tablespoons mayonnaise

¼ cup chopped scallions

¼ cup diced red bell peppers

¼ cup peeled and diced cucumbers

2 ripe Indian red peaches,
pitted and thinly sliced

8 leaves Boston lettuce,
coarsely chopped

METHOD—To prepare the dressing: Whisk together the yogurt, poppyseeds, jalapeño, orange juice, and ¼ cup of the lime juice until smooth, and season to taste with salt and pepper.

To prepare the crab: Mix together the crabmeat, the remaining ¼ cup lime juice, the mayonnaise, scallions, red bell peppers, and cucumbers. Season to taste with salt and pepper.

To prepare the peaches: Toss the peaches with half of the yogurt dressing.

ASSEMBLY—Place a mound of Boston lettuce in the center of each plate. Fan the peach slices on top of the lettuce and spoon the crab mixture in a ring around the lettuce. Drizzle the remaining yogurt dressing around the plate and top with freshly ground black pepper.

WINE NOTES—The delicate mineral flavors of Loire Valley Chenin Blancs pair perfectly with crab. Savennières from Domaine de Closel are especially good because they echo the delicate peach flavors in the salad.

GRILLED SWORDFISH AND SOMEN NOODLE SALAD WITH CILANTRO VINAIGRETTE

A lot of different types of seafood, including lobster, tuna, and salmon, can be successfully substituted for the swordfish in this recipe. I prefer swordfish for its meatiness and the way it stands up to the **assertiveness and straight-ahead intensity** of the blended cilantro vinaigrette. Somen or soba noodles provide substance and a soothing yet chewy texture, and the lettuce adds a cleansing effect. When the fish is hot off the grill, the temperature contrast adds an extra dimension to the dish.

SERVES 4

½ cup olive oil

¼ cup sesame oil

¼ cup canola oil

2 tablespoons rice wine vinegar

3 tablespoons freshly squeezed lemon juice

3 tablespoons freshly squeezed lime juice

2 tablespoons minced fresh ginger

1 tablespoon minced garlic

½ cup fresh cilantro leaves, chopped

2 tablespoons black sesame seeds

Salt and pepper

4 3-ounce swordfish fillets

8 ounces buckwheat somen noodles, cooked and chilled

3 cups shredded romaine lettuce

2 stalks celery, diced

¼ cup minced red onion

METHOD—To prepare the vinaigrette: Purée the olive, sesame, and canola oils, the rice wine vinegar, lemon juice, lime juice, ginger, garlic, cilantro, and sesame seeds until smooth, and season to taste with salt and pepper.

To prepare the swordfish: Season the swordfish with salt and pepper and brush with some of the vinaigrette. Grill over a moderate flame for 2 to 3 minutes on each side, or until the fish is cooked, and cool to room temperature.

To prepare the noodles: Toss the somen noodles, romaine, celery, and red onion with three-fourths of the remaining vinaigrette and season to taste with salt and pepper.

ASSEMBLY—Arrange some of the noodle mixture in the center of each plate. Place a piece of the swordfish on top of the noodles and spoon the remaining vinaigrette over the fish and around the plate. Top with freshly ground black pepper.

WINE NOTES—Aromatic, lean varietals such as Gruner Veltliner and Riesling from Austria are a seamless match to this dish. The Langeloiser "Spiegel" Gruner Veltliner from Loimer has enough racy acidity to cut through the rich swordfish.

Chapter

3

Lobster

LOBSTER TART WITH CHORIZO SAUSAGE AND
LOBSTER STOCK EMULSION

This preparation features chunks of lobster with spicy chorizo sausage.

The playful spiciness of the sausage

perfectly showcases the plump meatiness and natural sweetness of the lobster.

The tomato and spinach nicely cut into the rich lobster and sausage,

and the mushrooms add a pungence that gives the dish an overall earthiness.

Chicken could easily be substituted for the sausage,

and fettuccine or cappellini could be used

in place of the tart shell.

SERVES 4

1 teaspoon chopped shallots

1 teaspoon olive oil

¾ cup sliced button mushrooms

1 link chorizo sausage, sliced

Salt and pepper

2 cooked lobster tails, shelled

¼ cup plus 2 tablespoons butter

2 cups Shellfish Stock (see page 216)

4 Pâte Brisée Tart Shells
(recipe follows)

½ cup Braised Leeks (recipe follows)

8 cooked baby corn,
halved lengthwise

1½ cups fresh spinach leaves,
blanched

⅓ cup diced Olive Oil–Poached
Tomatoes (see page 210)

4 teaspoons Basil Oil (see page 198)

3 tablespoons fine basil chiffonade

METHOD—To prepare the tart filling: Cook the shallots in the olive oil in a medium sauté pan for 5 minutes, or until translucent. Add the mushrooms and cook for 2 minutes. Add the sliced chorizo and cook for 2 to 3 minutes, or until the sausage is heated through. Season to taste with salt and pepper and keep warm.

To prepare the lobster: Slice the lobster tails into ½-inch-thick medallions and place on a sheet pan. Cut 2 tablespoons of the butter into tiny pieces, place over the lobster pieces, and season the lobster to taste with salt and pepper. Place the lobster in a 350-degree oven for 3 minutes, or until just warm. (Be careful not to overcook the lobster or it will become chewy.)

To prepare the shellfish emulsion: Simmer the stock in a medium saucepan for 15 minutes, or until reduced to ¾ cup. Blend in the remaining ¼ cup butter with a handheld blender and season to taste with salt and pepper.

To assemble the tarts: Place the Pâte Brisée Tart Shells on a sheet pan. Place a bed of the Braised Leeks in the bottom of each tart shell, reserving 4 teaspoons. Arrange some of the lobster pieces, chorizo-mushroom mixture, baby corn, spinach, and Olive Oil–Poached Tomatoes on top of the leeks. Reheat the tarts at 350 degrees for 3 to 4 minutes, or until hot.

ASSEMBLY—Froth the emulsion with a handheld blender. Place 1 teaspoon of the reserved leeks in the center of each plate. Place a warm tart on top of the leeks. Spoon some of the shellfish emulsion over and around the tarts and drizzle with the Basil Oil. Sprinkle with the basil and top with black pepper.

WINE NOTES—The richness of an oaky Napa Valley Chardonnay such as Talbott or Au Bon Climat is the perfect balance for the spice of the chorizo and the delicate, buttery flavor of the tart but still allows the rich lobster to shine through. A more delicate style of rosé such as Pinot Noir or Grenache would also work well.

Pâte Brisée Tart Shells

This dough will keep for several months in your freezer.

YIELD: 4-6 TART SHELLS

1¼ cups flour
2 tablespoons sugar
¾ teaspoon salt
⅔ cup cold butter, cubed
1 egg yolk
3 tablespoons ice water

METHOD—Mix the flour, sugar, salt, and butter in an electric mixer on low speed until the ingredients are combined and the butter is in pea-sized chunks. Add the egg yolk and water all at once and mix on low speed until the dough just begins to come together. Remove the dough to a lightly floured work surface and form it into a ball. Cover the dough in plastic wrap and refrigerate for at least 30 minutes.

Roll the dough out on a lightly floured surface to ⅛ inch thick and cut into four 5-inch circles. Press the dough into four 3-inch-diameter by ½-inch-high tart rings and place the rings on a parchment-lined sheet pan. Bake at 350 degrees for 15 minutes, or until golden brown. Let cool on the pan, and carefully remove the tart rings. (Extra dough may be frozen.)

Braised Leeks

These leeks can be puréed with a little chicken stock and served as leek soup.

YIELD: ABOUT ¾ CUP

1 leek, cut into ¼-inch-thick pieces
2 tablespoons butter
1 cup Chicken Stock (see page 201)

METHOD—Cook the leeks and butter in a medium saucepan over medium-low heat for 10 minutes, or until translucent. Add the stock and cook over medium-low heat for 30 minutes, or until the leeks are very soft and most of the liquid is absorbed. Season to taste with salt and pepper.

TROPICAL FRUIT AND LOBSTER SALAD WITH BLACK PEPPER–VANILLA BEAN VINAIGRETTE

The sweetness and acid present in most tropical fruits are a tremendous complement
to the lush meatiness of lobster or other shellfish such as shrimp or scallops.
The Black Pepper–Vanilla Bean Vinaigrette
provides a tropical sensuality and pleasant, cutting heat, and
watercress adds the cleansing quality
needed to keep the fruit, lobster, and vinaigrette in perfect balance.
This dish would be great for an outdoor luncheon on a hot summer day.

SERVES 4

2 1-pound lobsters, boiled and shelled

Black Pepper–Vanilla Bean Vinaigrette (see page 200)

Salt and pepper

4 cups watercress

1 guava

½ mango, peeled, pitted, and cut into ⅛-inch-thick slices

⅛ papaya, peeled, seeded, and cut into ⅛-inch-thick slices

1 cup ⅛-inch-thick pineapple wedges

¼ cup tiny fresh mint leaves

1 passion fruit, halved and pulp reserved

METHOD—To prepare the lobster: Cut the lobster claws in half and slice the lobster tail into ½-inch-thick medallions. Toss the lobster meat with enough of the Black Pepper–Vanilla Bean Vinaigrette to coat the lobster. Season to taste with salt and pepper.

To prepare the watercress: Toss the watercress with 1 tablespoon of the Black Pepper–Vanilla Bean Vinaigrette and season to taste with salt and pepper.

To prepare the guava: Cut the peel off of the guava keeping the natural shape intact. Cut thin slices from the outside of the guava, removing any seeds from the guava slices.

To prepare the salad: Toss together the watercress, mango, papaya, pineapple, and guava in a small bowl.

peeled guava with top cut off

cut away thin slices

ASSEMBLY—Place some of the salad in the center of each plate. Arrange the lobster knuckle and tail meat down the center of the salad and top with a lobster claw half. Sprinkle a few of the mint leaves around the plates and spoon some of the Black Pepper–Vanilla Bean Vinaigrette over the lobster and around the plates. Spoon the passion fruit pulp around the plates.

WINE NOTES—The citrus and toasty oak flavors of most white Bordeaux are a wonderful balance to tropical fruit flavors. Producers such as Prieure-Lichine and Pavillon Blanc du Château Margaux have an aromatic grapefruit flavor and great acidity that is a wonderful pair with this salad.

LOBSTER AND BRAISED ENDIVE WITH HORSERADISH POTATOES

This hearty dish boasts unforgettable flavors and satisfies in every way.

Creamy potatoes with their horseradish-induced bite

and sharp, braised endive perfectly offset the meaty, sensuous lobster.

Meat stock reduction provides another layer of richness altogether,

firmly pushing this dish into red wine territory.

Salmon or tuna could easily be used in place of the lobster, and a sauté or ragout

of mushrooms would be the perfect accompaniment to this

most satisfying combination of flavors.

SERVES 4

¼ cup chopped carrots

¼ cup chopped celery

½ cup chopped onions

1 tablespoon canola oil

1 tablespoon sugar

2 small heads Belgian endive

Salt and pepper

1 Idaho potato, peeled, boiled, and riced

⅓ cup finely grated fresh horseradish

¼ cup plus 2 tablespoons butter

½ cup heavy cream

2 1½-pound lobsters, boiled and shelled

2 tablespoons chopped fresh chives

¼ cup hot Meat Stock Reduction (see page 208)

METHOD—To prepare the endive: Place the carrots, celery, and onions in a small saucepan with the canola oil and cook for 3 to 4 minutes, or until the vegetables are caramelized. Add the sugar and endive and enough water to cover two-thirds of the endive. Cover with a lid and simmer for 20 minutes, or until the endive is tender. Remove the endive from the liquid, cut each head into quarters lengthwise, and season to taste with salt and pepper.

To prepare the horseradish potatoes: Rewarm the potatoes, if necessary. Whip the warm riced potatoes, horseradish, and ¼ cup of the butter with an electric mixer until smooth. Add the cream, whip until incorporated, and season to taste with salt and pepper. (Additional cream may be added, if necessary, to make the potatoes loose enough to spoon into a ring shape.) Keep warm until ready to use.

To prepare the lobster: Cut the lobster claws in half lengthwise and slice the tail into ½-inch-thick medallions. Sauté the lobster in 2 tablespoons butter for 2 to 3 minutes, or until hot. Add the chives and season with salt and pepper.

ASSEMBLY—Place 2 pieces of the braised endive in the center of each plate. Arrange some of the lobster meat over the endive and spoon the potato purée into a ring around the endive. Spoon the Meat Stock Reduction over the lobster and inside the potato ring and top with freshly ground black pepper.

WINE NOTES—The acidity and delicate heat of the horseradish calls for a delicate red with very ripe fruit characteristics. A new World Syrah from Qupe or Ojai will have the rich, ripe fruit necessary for the horseradish, but still allow the delicate lobster shine through.

LOBSTER WITH ORZO, ASPARAGUS, AND SAFFRON TOMATO SAUCE

This light but satisfying dish works nicely as either an appetizer or an entrée

by simply adjusting portion size.

The plump lobster meat and the toothsome orzo

are perfectly balanced by the cleansing asparagus and the zesty Saffron Tomato Sauce.

Chicken or beef would work well in place of the lobster.

If you like a little heat,

try spicing up the tomato sauce with a few chile peppers.

SERVES 4

½ cup Pickling Juice (see page 211)

½ cup julienned red onions

3 cups cooked orzo

3 tablespoons olive oil

½ cup chopped green onions

½ cup julienned sundried tomatoes

Salt and pepper

4 small par-boiled lobster tails, shelled and halved lengthwise

1 tablespoon butter

12 asparagus spears, blanched

Saffron Tomato Sauce (see page 215)

2 tablespoons chopped fresh basil leaves

METHOD—To prepare the onions: Place the Pickling Juice over medium heat for 3 minutes, or until warm. Add the red onions, remove from the heat, and let stand for 30 minutes. Strain the onions from the juice. (The juice can be stored in the refrigerator for another use.)

To prepare the orzo: Heat the orzo with the olive oil, green onions, and sundried tomatoes over medium heat for 5 minutes, or until warm. Season to taste with salt and pepper.

To prepare the lobster: Sauté the lobster in the butter over medium heat for 1 minute on each side, or until light golden brown. Season to taste with salt and pepper.

ASSEMBLY—Arrange 3 asparagus spears in the center of each plate and top with a large spoonful of the orzo. Overlap 2 of the lobster pieces on top of the orzo and arrange some of the pickled red onions over the lobster. Spoon the Saffron Tomato Sauce around the plates and sprinkle with the basil.

WINE NOTES—Condrieu from the northern Rhone Valley has an elegant richness that will perfectly accompany this lobster. It has intensely floral aromatics that make the saffron seem to stand out. Producers such as Guigal and Vernay are delicious examples, and both are fairly easy to find.

LOBSTER EN BARIGOULE

This dish, which originated in the south of France, has delicate overtones,

yet it simultaneously has a lot of presence!

The braised artichokes, carrots, and onions mingle in an elegant broth

that is subtly sweetened with tarragon. I use lobster instead of the traditional red snapper because

I enjoy the richness and decadence

it creates. While potatoes and haricots verts are not found in original barigoules,

they fit in nicely and provide enough substance

to make this dish a meal in itself.

SERVES 4

½ cup chopped carrots

½ cup chopped celery

1½ cloves garlic, chopped

1 cup chopped onions

2 tablespoons canola oil

12 baby artichokes, trimmed

¾ cup plus 2 tablespoons butter

1 lemon, halved

2 quarts Chicken Stock (see page 201)

1 small Spanish onion

½ cup white wine

1½ cups sliced carrots

3 cups fingerling (or small red or white) potatoes

1 cup blanched haricots verts, cut into 1-inch-diagonal-cut pieces

1 tablespoon rice wine vinegar

¼ cup fresh tarragon leaves, chopped

¼ cup fresh parsley leaves, chopped

Salt and pepper

4 small lobster tails, boiled, shelled, and sliced into medallions

¼ cup Red Bell Pepper Mayonnaise (recipe follows)

METHOD—To prepare the artichokes: Cook the chopped carrots, celery, garlic, and onions in the canola oil in a large saucepan for 3 to 5 minutes, or until the vegetables are caramelized. Add the baby artichokes, ¼ cup of the butter, and the lemon halves, and cover with the stock. Place a towel or a piece of parchment paper over the pan to cover. Bring the liquid to a slow simmer and cook for 15 to 20 minutes, or until the artichokes are tender. Remove the artichokes from the liquid and set aside to cool. Strain the liquid, discarding the solids, and set the liquid aside. Slice the artichokes in half lengthwise (or into bite-sized pieces if using larger artichokes).

To prepare the potatoes: Peel the potatoes and boil in salted water for 7 to 10 minutes, or until just cooked. Drain the water and cut the potatoes into bite-sized wedges.

To prepare the barigoule: Cut the Spanish onion into thick strips and sweat in 2 tablespoons of the butter in a large saucepan over medium heat for 3 to 4 minutes, or until the onions are translucent. Add the white wine and cook for 5 minutes, or until reduced by half. Add the sliced carrots, the potatoes wedges, haricots verts, artichokes, and the reserved cooking liquid from the artichokes. Bring the liquid to a simmer and add the rice wine vinegar, tarragon, and parsley. Whisk in the remaining ½ cup butter and season to taste with salt and pepper.

To warm the lobster: Place the lobster medallions on a sheet pan and heat in the oven at 350 degrees for 2 to 3 minutes, or until warm.

ASSEMBLY—Ladle some of the barigoule into each bowl. Arrange some of the lobster in each bowl and place 1 tablespoon of the Red Bell Pepper Mayonnaise over the lobster. Top with freshly ground black pepper.

WINE NOTES—This dish requires a wine with enough acidity to balance the sweetness of the rouille, and enough richness to offset the acidity of the artichokes. A high-acid Chardonnay with toasty oak by Mount Eden Vineyards will mesh beautifully with this dish.

Red Bell Pepper Mayonnaise

If you don't have a juicer, the pieces of roasted red bell pepper can be puréed with the mayonnaise.

YIELD: ABOUT ¾ CUP

2 red bell peppers, juiced
½ cup mayonnaise
Salt and pepper

METHOD—Simmer the bell pepper juice over medium heat for 10 to 15 minutes, or until reduced to ¼ cup. Remove from the heat and refrigerate for 30 minutes, or until cool. Purée the reduced juice into the mayonnaise until completely combined. Season to taste with salt and pepper.

This is a highly versatile preparation in terms of how it can be served and what can be added to it.

It can be prepared in advance and served cold, warm, or hot.

With a piece of fish hot off the grill placed right on top of the lobster-strewn tabbouleh, it becomes a perfect main course

or side course for dinner.

The spicy Apricot Curry Sauce

provides clean, light, and refreshing notes, with flavors that magnificently complement the succulent morsels of lobster.

Try folding in pieces of sautéed mushrooms, or even scoop the tabbouleh

onto a mound of greens to create a glorious salad.

SERVES 4

2 cups cooked cracked bulgur wheat, chilled

½ cup small-diced cucumbers

2 tablespoons mint chiffonade

3 tablespoons chopped
fresh parsley leaves

½ cup diced tomatoes

¼ cup small-diced
Granny Smith apple

¼ cup diced dried apricots

1 boiled lobster tail, shelled and diced

3 tablespoons olive oil

3 tablespoons freshly squeezed
orange juice

1 teaspoon Togarashi (see page 219)

Salt and pepper

Apricot Curry Sauce (see page 198)

METHOD—To prepare the tabbouleh salad: Mix together the cracked bulgur wheat, cucumbers, mint, parsley, tomato, apple, apricots, lobster, olive oil, orange juice, and Togarashi in a large bowl and season to taste with salt and pepper.

ASSEMBLY—Place a large spoonful of the tabbouleh in the center of each plate and spoon the Apricot Curry Sauce around the plates. Top with freshly ground black pepper.

WINE NOTES—Leaner varietals such as Austrian Gruner Veltliner or a crisp style Sonoma Sauvignon Blanc are a must for Tabbouleh. The Togarashi in this dish adds a delicate heat element that the acicity of these wines seems to cleanse away.

tabbouleh

lobster claw

apricot curry sauce

Chapter

4

Scallop

SAUTÉED SCALLOPS WITH BRAISED LEGUMES, CRISPY LEEKS, AND RED WINE VINAIGRETTE

This hearty dish is also quite refined. The plump scallops come across as even more lush than they normally do against the buttery legumes, and the red wine vinaigrette is appropriately light in body but contains enough fruity acid to cut into the two feature components. For convenience, the legumes can be cooked a day or two ahead, and the entire dish can be assembled in just a few minutes.

SERVES 4

¾ cup red kidney beans

¾ cup cranberry beans

¾ cup cannellini beans

2 cups chopped onions

1 cup chopped carrots

1 cup chopped celery

2 tablespoons plus 1 teaspoon canola oil

3 tablespoons butter

3 small sprigs rosemary

4 cups Chicken Stock (see page 201)

Salt and pepper

1 leek, cleaned and cut into ⅛-inch-thick rings

3 tablespoons flour

Canola oil for frying

2 tablespoons minced shallots

¼ cup olive oil

3 cups red wine

2 tablespoons chopped fresh chives

¼ cup olive oil

8 large sea scallops

METHOD—To prepare the legumes: Soak the beans overnight in separate bowls of water. Drain the water from the beans. Divide the onions, carrots, and celery among three small saucepans and add 1 teaspoon of the canola oil to each pan. Place each pan over medium heat and cook for 5 to 7 minutes, or until golden brown and caramelized. Add one kind of bean to each saucepan. Add 1 tablespoon of the butter, 1 sprig of the rosemary, and 1⅓ cup of the stock to each saucepan. Gently simmer the beans for 45 to 90 minutes, or until tender (the larger beans will take much longer to cook than the smaller ones). Add water in small amounts if the stock is absorbed before the beans are tender. When the beans are cooked, remove the rosemary sprigs and any large vegetable chunks. Combine all of the braised legumes into one large saucepan and season to taste with salt and pepper. Keep warm until ready to use.

To prepare the fried leeks: Toss the leek rings in the flour, dusting off any excess, and season with pepper. Fry the leek rings in canola oil heated to 350 degrees for 30 to 60 seconds, or until golden brown and crispy. Blot on paper towels and season to taste with salt.

To prepare the vinaigrette: Sweat the shallots in 1 tablespoon of the olive oil over medium heat for 30 to 45 seconds, or until translucent. Add the red wine and cook for 30 to 45 minutes, or until reduced to about ⅓ cup. Add the chives and slowly whisk the remaining 3 tablespoons of olive oil into the pan. Season to taste with salt and pepper.

To prepare the scallops: Season the scallops with salt and pepper. Quickly sauté the scallops over medium-high heat with the remaining 1 tablespoon canola oil for 2 minutes on each side, or until just cooked. Remove the scallops from the pan and keep warm.

ASSEMBLY—Place some of the braised legumes in the center of each plate. Arrange 2 scallops over the legumes. Spoon the vinaigrette around the plate and place some of the crispy leeks over the scallops.

WINE NOTES—The braised legumes add a richness to this dish that can only be cleansed by a lightly tart red wine. Swanson Vineyard Sangiovese from Napa Valley has a tart cherry finish that perfectly cuts through the richness of these legumes.

SCALLOPS IN FILO WITH SPINACH,
PORTOBELLO MUSHROOMS, AND CURRY EMULSION

This is a fun dish for a slightly more upscale presentation. It is actually simpler to assemble the scallops in filo than it may appear, but in the interest of saving time, the filo process can be omitted and the scallops can be served on a bed of the mushrooms and spinach with the sauce spooned over the top. However, the extra step of wrapping the scallops in filo results in a far more complex textural effect because the scallops stay especially moist (indeed they are almost steamed) when contained in filo, and the pastry provides a satisfying richness.

SERVES 4

4 large sea scallops

4 Roasted Portobello Mushrooms
(see page 214)

3 tablespoons olive oil

Salt and pepper

3 sheets filo dough

¼ cup melted butter

1 cup Chicken Stock (see page 201)

2 tablespoons freshly squeezed
lemon juice

3 tablespoons Curry Butter
(recipe follows)

1 tablespoon minced shallots

2 teaspoons butter

2 cups fresh spinach leaves, blanched

½ cup Granny Smith apple batons
with skin on

2 tablespoons fresh basil leaves,
cut into chiffonade

METHOD—To prepare the scallops: Cut each scallop into 4 discs. Cut the Roasted Portobello Mushrooms into discs the same size as the scallops and cut each disc into 3 thin slices. Julienne the remaining portobello pieces and set aside. Rub the scallop slices with the olive oil and season the scallop and portobello mushroom slices with salt and pepper. Layer the scallop and portobello mushroom slices in 4 stacks, each containing 4 alternating layers of scallop and 3 layers of portobello mushroom. Cover with plastic wrap and refrigerate until needed.

Lay out a sheet of filo dough and brush with the melted butter. Top with another sheet of filo dough and brush with melted butter. Top with another sheet of filo and brush with melted butter. Cut the filo stack into four 5-inch squares. Place 1 of the scallop-mushroom stacks in the center of each filo square. Carefully fold in the corners, completely enclosing the stacks in the filo dough. Place the packages on a parchment-lined sheet pan with the seam side down. Brush the tops with the remaining butter and refrigerate for 30 minutes. Bake at 450 degrees for 10 to 12 minutes, or until the filo is golden brown and crispy.

To prepare the emulsion: Bring the Chicken Stock and lemon juice to a simmer and remove from the heat. Slowly whisk in the Curry Butter and season to taste with salt and pepper.

61

To prepare the mushrooms: Sauté the reserved julienned portobello mushrooms and the shallots in the butter over medium-high heat for 3 minutes, or until hot and season to taste with salt and pepper.

ASSEMBLY—Place some of the spinach, sautéed mushrooms, and apple in the center of each plate. Slice each of the scallop en croutes in half and place both halves on top of the mushrooms. Spoon the curry butter emulsion around the plate and sprinkle with the basil. Top with freshly ground black pepper.

WINE NOTES—A richer Pinot Gris from Alsace by Kuentz-Bas or Domaine Zind Humbrecht will balance well with the scallops and have the delicate aroma of white pepper, which is a wonderful complement with the spinach in this dish.

Curry Butter

This butter is also great for making curried croutons.

YIELD: ABOUT ½ CUP

¼ cup peeled and chopped Granny Smith apple

1 clove garlic

1 shallot, chopped

1 teaspoon canola oil

2 teaspoons curry powder

½ teaspoon paprika

2 tablespoons water

¼ cup butter, at room temperature

METHOD—Sauté the apple, garlic, and shallot in the canola oil over medium heat for 7 minutes. Add the curry powder, paprika, and water and cook for 3 minutes. Let cool and fold in the butter. Purée until smooth and strain through a fine-mesh sieve. Refrigerate until ready to use or for up to 3 days, or keep in the freezer for up to 2 months.

BAY SCALLOP CEVICHE WITH STAR ANISE
AND CITRUS JUICE

This delicate ceviche could either be served as a main course for lunch or as a superb appetizer before a chicken or steak dinner. This preparation has several virtues beyond its fabulous flavor— it is light and healthy, it can be made several hours ahead, and it can be served in any portion size. The star anise and citrus are highly complementary, and they also showcase the delicate bay scallops. Pieces of tropical fruit, such as mango, papaya, or pineapple, or a handful of mesclun could be added to make this a more substantial dish.

SERVES 4

½ cup freshly squeezed orange juice

¼ cup freshly squeezed lime juice

¼ cup freshly squeezed lemon juice

½ teaspoon ground star anise

32 bay scallops

Salt and pepper

½ cup olive oil

½ cup Pickling Juice (see page 211)

¼ cup finely julienned red onion

4 tablespoons fresh parsley sprigs

4 tablespoons fresh chervil sprigs

3 tablespoons fresh dill sprigs

3 tablespoons fresh small basil sprigs

4 oranges

1½ cups small-diced watermelon

METHOD—To prepare the ceviche: Combine the orange, lime, and lemon juices and the star anise and fold in the scallops. Cover and refrigerate for 45 minutes, folding gently every 10 minutes to distribute the juices. Remove from the refrigerator, season with salt and pepper, and remove the scallops from the liquid and set aside. Whisk the olive oil into the liquid, and season with salt and pepper.

To prepare the pickled onions: Cook the Pickling Juice over medium heat for 5 minutes, or until warm. Remove from the heat, add the red onions, and refrigerate for 30 minutes, or until cool. Strain the onions from the Pickling Juice.

To prepare the herbs: Toss the parsley, chervil, dill, and basil with 3 tablespoons of the liquid from the ceviche, and season to taste with salt and pepper.

To prepare the oranges: Cut the tops and bottoms from the oranges. Cut the peel, retaining the orange's natural shape. Cut along both sides of each membrane, removing the orange segments, and discarding the membranes.

ASSEMBLY—Arrange the orange segments in the center of each plate. Spoon the watermelon in the center of the oranges and top with the herbs. Sprinkle some of the red onions around the plate and spoon the scallop ceviche over the herbs. Spoon the reserved ceviche juice over the scallops and around the plate. Top with freshly ground black pepper.

WINE NOTES—Duckhorn or Spottswoode Sauvignon Blancs are an incredible pairing for this dish. The sweet fennel flavors in the wines are echoed by the star anise in the dish, yet both wines have enough acidity to balance with the ceviche without hiding the delicate flavor of the bay scallops.

64

PINWHEEL OF SCALLOP WITH CUMIN-SCENTED FETTUCCINE AND HEIRLOOM TOMATO SAUCE

Pinwheeled scallops make a truly beautiful presentation, plus it's easy to do. The glistening, golden brown surface reveals the majesty of the greatest of all mollusks. Here, the scallop pinwheel sits on a mound of exotically flavored pasta and is served with a slightly sweet and barely acidic Heirloom Tomato Sauce for an extraordinary balance of textures and flavors. Consuming this preparation is highly sensual, with a richness of flavor that belies a fairly light dish. The scallops can be cooked whole instead of pinwheeled if you are short on time.

SERVES 4

2 teaspoons cumin seeds, toasted and crushed

1 tablespoon minced shallots

2 tablespoons red wine vinegar

½ cup plus 2 tablespoons olive oil

Salt and pepper

8 ounces fresh fettuccine, cooked

1 cup diced Spanish onions

3 cloves garlic, minced

3 large yellow heirloom tomatoes, peeled, seeded, and chopped

1 tablespoon Spicy Vinegar (see page 215)

8 sea scallops, thinly sliced

4 teaspoons butter

2 tablespoons fresh chives cut into 1-inch pieces on the diagonal

METHOD—To prepare the fettuccine: Place the cumin seeds, shallots, and red wine vinegar in a small bowl and slowly whisk in ½ cup of the olive oil. Season to taste with salt and pepper. Add the warm fettuccine and toss.

To prepare the tomato sauce: Sweat the onions and garlic with the remaining 2 tablespoons olive oil for 5 minutes, or until the onions are translucent. Add the tomatoes and Spicy Vinegar and cook for 20 minutes over medium heat. Purée the sauce until smooth and season to taste with salt and pepper.

To prepare the scallops: Divide the scallops into 4 portions. Cut four 3-inch circles of parchment paper and butter one side. Overlap the scallop slices to form 2½-inch pinwheels on the buttered side of the parchment. Season with salt and pepper. Place 1 teaspoon of butter in a hot nonstick sauté pan and invert a scallop pinwheel into the pan with the parchment side up. Cook for 1 minute, remove the parchment paper, and cook for 30 seconds. Turn over the pinwheels, cook for 20 seconds, or until just cooked. Repeat with the remaining scallop pinwheels.

ASSEMBLY—Spread a circle of the heirloom tomato sauce in the center of each plate. Mound the fettuccine on the sauce and top with a scallop pinwheel. Sprinkle with the chives and top with freshly ground black pepper.

WINE NOTES—The rich, ripe fruit of a Talbott Chardonnay from Monterey is the perfect balance for the sweetness of the scallops and the spice of the cumin. The integrated oakiness of the wine accentuates the caramelized scallops, and the delicate acidity brings out the sweetness of the tomato sauce.

SCALLOP-CRAB CAKES WITH HOT AND SOUR
MANGO SLICES AND CILANTRO JUICE

Most people are familiar with crab cakes, but this preparation offers a refreshing twist. These are made **lighter and more interesting** by combining roughly equal parts of crab and scallops. The cakes are served on sliced hot-and-sour mangoes for an **incredibly explosive flavor** and a glorious flavor contrast. An aromatic cilantro juice is drizzled on the plate, providing an **extraordinary balance to the cakes and the mango.** Because there is none of the cream or butter sauce that is typically served with crab cakes, the clean, unmuted taste of the seafood shines through.

SERVES 4

1 cup Pickling Juice (see page 211)

1 cup thinly sliced mango

4 sea scallops, chopped

¼ cup heavy cream

1 egg white

1 cup crabmeat

1 cup bread crumbs

½ cup small-diced red bell peppers

½ cup small-diced
yellow bell peppers

3 tablespoons chopped
fresh cilantro leaves

½ cup chopped scallions

2 tablespoons minced shallots

½ teaspoon Togarashi (see page 219)

Salt and pepper

2 tablespoons canola oil

Cilantro Juice (recipe follows)

METHOD—To prepare the hot-and-sour mango slices: Pour the Pickling Juice over the mango slices, cover, and refrigerate for at least 1 hour.

To prepare the scallop-crab cakes: Purée the scallops, heavy cream, and egg white until smooth. Fold in the crabmeat, ½ cup of the bread crumbs, the red and yellow bell peppers, cilantro, scallions, shallots, and Togarashi, and season with salt and pepper. Cover with plastic wrap and refrigerate for 1 hour.

Form the scallop mixture into eight 1-inch-thick patties and dredge each cake in the remaining bread crumbs. Place the canola oil in a large, hot, nonstick sauté pan over medium heat, add the scallop-crab cakes, and cook for 2 to 3 minutes on each side, or until golden brown and crispy.

scallop crab cakes

hot & sour
mango slices

cilantro
juice

ASSEMBLY—Drain the mango from the Pickling Juice and arrange some of the slices in the center of each plate. Place 2 warm scallop-crab cakes over the mango slices and spoon the Cilantro Juice around the plate.

WINE NOTES—The lingering spice flavors and the sweetness from the tropical fruit both demand high acidity and delicate fruit. A lightly oaked Chardonnay, such as Matanzas Creek, or a Blancs de Blancs style of Champagne from Schramsberg would both be great matches.

Cilantro Juice

If the flavor of cilantro is too intense for you, use equal parts of parsley and cilantro.

YIELD: ABOUT ½ CUP

2 cups packed fresh cilantro leaves, blanched

3 tablespoons water

2 tablespoons canola oil

2 tablespoons olive oil

Salt and pepper

METHOD—Squeeze any excess water from the cilantro and purée with the water and oils for 3 to 4 minutes, or until smooth. Strain through a fine-mesh sieve and season to taste with salt and pepper. Refrigerate until ready to use, or for up to 8 hours.

SEA SCALLOPS WITH BLENDED CHICKEN LIVER SAUCE AND BRAISED COLLARD GREENS

With the heady and unusual flavor provided by the Chicken Liver Sauce, it is probably safe to say that this dish will find its greatest appreciation among the most sophisticated diners. You will be stunned by this wonderful combination of disparate but complementary flavors—the sweet scallops paired with slightly astringent collard greens and rich Chicken Liver Sauce. You will be surprised at how simple this dish is to put together, especially if the collard greens are prepared in advance. Also, tuna, swordfish, or even chicken would be great substitutions for the scallops.

SERVES 4

¼ cup chopped uncooked bacon

1 cup chopped onions

4 chicken livers

Salt and pepper

2 tablespoons butter

1 cup Madeira

1 cup Chicken Stock (see page 201)

4 cups chopped collard greens

½ teaspoon sugar

1 tablespoon balsamic vinegar

8 sea scallops

2 tablespoons canola oil

2 tablespoons plus 2 teaspoons aged balsamic vinegar (at least 12 years old)

METHOD—To prepare the sauce: Sauté 2 tablespoons of the bacon with the onion for 3 to 4 minutes, or until the onions are caramelized. Season the chicken livers with salt and pepper. Add the butter to the sauté pan and push the onions and bacon to the side of the pan. Add the chicken livers, and cook for 3 to 4 minutes, or until golden brown. Add ¾ cup of the Madeira and cook for 3 minutes, or until the wine is reduced by half. Purée the chicken liver mixture and stock until smooth and strain through a fine-mesh sieve. Cook the sauce for 5 minutes, or until warm. Season to taste with salt and pepper.

To prepare the collard greens: Sauté the remaining 2 tablespoons bacon over medium-low heat for 2 minutes, or until most of the fat is rendered. Add the collard greens and cook for 3 minutes. Add the remaining ¼ cup Madeira and cook for 4 minutes. Add the sugar and balsamic vinegar and cook for 2 to 3 minutes, or until the collard greens are tender. Season to taste with salt and pepper

To prepare the scallops: Season the scallops with salt and pepper. Place the canola oil in a hot sauté pan, add the scallops, and cook over medium heat for 2 minutes on each side, or until the scallops are lightly browned and just cooked.

ASSEMBLY—Spread a circle of the chicken liver sauce on each plate. Place the collard greens on the sauce and top with 2 scallops. Drizzle the aged balsamic vinegar around the plates and top with freshly ground black pepper.

WINE NOTES—The richness of the chicken liver sauce requires an earthy style of Barbera from Italy such as Giacomo Conterno's Barbera d'Alba. Its delicate earthiness and rich fruit will not cover the delicate flavors of the scallop.

Chapter

5

Catfish

CATFISH TEMPURA WITH LEMONGRASS–JALAPEÑO–PONZU DIPPING SAUCE

Deep-frying heavily-breaded catfish has a tendency to obscure the delicate flavor of the fish. But using a light batter and quickly frying in very hot oil, as is done here, results in a crispy exterior, yet allows the flavor and richness of the fish to shine through. The spicy ponzu dipping sauce is served alongside to cut the richness of the catfish. This preparation works well as either an appetizer or an entrée.

SERVES 4

8 ounces ponzu sauce

1 stalk lemongrass,
shaved into thin rings

1 jalapeño, thinly sliced

1¼ cups flour

2½ teaspoons baking powder

1 egg

½ cup plus 2 tablespoons water

Salt and pepper

½ cup plus 2 tablespoons egg whites
(about 5)

4 cups canola oil

12 1-ounce strips catfish

1 small sweet potato, peeled and sliced
crosswise into ⅛-inch-thick discs

4 scallions, cut in half lengthwise

1 small Japanese eggplant,
cut crosswise into ⅛-inch-thick discs

8 small button mushrooms

1 small yellow squash, cut crosswise
into ⅛-inch-thick discs

1 small zucchini, cut crosswise into
⅛-inch-thick discs

1 teaspoon Togarashi (see page 219)

2 tablespoons julienned
fresh cilantro leaves

METHOD—To prepare the dipping sauce: Place the ponzu sauce, lemongrass, and jalapeño in a small saucepan and simmer for 5 minutes. Keep warm until ready to use.

To prepare the tempura: Place the flour and baking powder in a large mixing bowl. Whisk in the egg and water and season to taste with salt and pepper. Whip the egg whites until medium-stiff peaks form. Fold the egg whites into the flour mixture. (The tempura batter must be used within 15 minutes after the addition of the egg whites.)

Preheat the canola oil to 375 degrees in a large saucepan or wok. Season the catfish pieces with salt and pepper. In small batches, dip the catfish pieces, sweet potato, scallions, eggplant, mushrooms, squash, and zucchini into the tempura batter, completely coating each ingredient. Place the coated vegetables and fish into the oil and cook for 2 minutes on each side, or until golden brown. Drain on paper towels and season with salt and pepper and the Togarashi. Keep warm in a 225-degree oven until all of the catfish and vegetables are cooked.

ASSEMBLY—Divide the dipping sauce into 4 small ramekins or bowls. Arrange some of the tempura in the center of each plate and sprinkle with the julienned cilantro.

WINE NOTES—Champagne is the perfect companion for the salt flavors in the sauce, and it refreshes the palate after the fried tempura. But, for something fun and different, try one of the many available boutique Asian beers.

WOK-SMOKED CATFISH WITH SWEET-AND-SOUR FENNEL AND KUMQUAT SAUCE

Smoked catfish is a special treat, especially when served hot off the smoker,

and it is actually fairly easy to prepare. In this simple setup the fish is smoked

in a wok right on the stove. As the catfish is smoked it is also cooking very slowly,

resulting in incredibly succulent flesh.

The sweet and sour fennel provides both a crunchy texture and a great flavor contrast

to the buttery, smoky fish. The tangy kumquat sauce provides further contrast to the luscious catfish.

This preparation would also

work wonderfully with chicken or scallops.

SERVES 4

4 3-ounce pieces catfish

1½ cups Pickling Juice (see page 211)

3 cups hickory chips

10 kumquats

2 tablespoons sugar

1 small bulb fennel, julienned

¾ cup raisins

1 large pear, peeled, cored, and diced

3 tablespoons chopped fennel tops

¼ cup olive oil

1 tablespoon tangerine juice

3 sprigs thyme

1 tablespoon canola oil

Salt and pepper

2 tangerines, peeled, sectioned, and membranes removed

METHOD—To prepare the fish for smoking: Place the catfish in a small container, cover with 1 cup of the Pickling Juice, and refrigerate overnight.

Cover 1 cup of the hickory chips with water and soak overnight.

To prepare the kumquat sauce: Place the kumquats in a small saucepan, cover with water, and simmer for 5 minutes. Drain the water and repeat the process three times. Add the sugar to the pan and cover the kumquats with water. Simmer the kumquats for 15 minutes and remove from the heat. Remove the kumquats from the pan, reserving the cooking liquid. Cut the kumquats in half and discard the pulp and seeds. Purée the skins with enough of the reserved cooking liquid to form a smooth sauce. Place the purée in a small saucepan and warm over medium heat, adding additional cooking liquid, if necessary, to thin to a sauce consistency.

To prepare the sweet-and-sour fennel: Cook the remaining ½ cup Pickling Juice and fennel in a small saucepan over low heat until just warm. Remove from the heat, add the raisins and pears, and fold in the fennel tops.

To prepare the vinaigrette: Whisk together the olive oil, tangerine juice, 2 teaspoons of the fennel tops, and 1 tablespoon of the fennel liquid. Season to taste with salt and pepper.

To prepare the smoked catfish: Place the remaining 2 cups hickory chips and the thyme sprigs in the bottom of a wok. Cover the wok and place on the stove over high heat for 10 minutes, or until the hickory chips start to smoke. Sprinkle the wet hickory chips over the dry ones, top with a wire rack, and cover with the wok lid.

Remove the catfish from the Pickling Juice and brush with the canola oil. Place the catfish on the wire rack, cover, and smoke for 5 to 7 minutes, or until the fish is just cooked. Carefully remove the catfish from the wok and serve immediately.

ASSEMBLY—Arrange some of the tangerine slices in the center of each plate. Place some of the sweet-and-sour fennel on the tangerines and top with a piece of the smoked catfish. Spoon the kumquat purée in a ring around the tangerines and spoon the vinaigrette over the catfish.

WINE NOTES—The ripe citrus fruit flavors of a New Zealand Sauvignon Blanc are gorgeous with the kumquat purée and the catfish, and at the same time the delicate fennel and caraway flavors of the wine accentuate those in the dish. Try a Sauvignon Blanc by Cloudy Bay or Villa Maria.

STEAMED CATFISH WITH WHITE NAVY BEANS AND HERB PURÉE

This is a twist on a traditional southern dish, with rich, earthy white navy beans providing the perfect backdrop for the moist, succulent catfish. The elegance of the steamed catfish is a dramatic contrast to the hamhock-flavored, buttery navy beans, and the vibrant, refreshing herb purée cuts beautifully into both the catfish and the beans. The navy beans can be made up to several days ahead; the herb purée can be made up to two hours ahead and then reheated just before serving.

SERVES 4

½ ounce whole fresh chives plus 2 tablespoons chopped

½ ounce fresh flat-leaf parsley

½ ounce fresh tarragon

¼ cup canola oil

¼ cup olive oil

½ cup ice water

Salt and pepper

8 baby carrots, peeled

2 cups Brussels sprouts, halved

1 zucchini, diced

3 tablespoons butter

1 cup water

4 4-ounce pieces catfish

Hamhock-flavored White Navy Beans (see page 206)

METHOD—To make the herb purée: Sauté the whole chives, the parsley, and tarragon in 2 tablespoons of the canola oil over high heat for 1½ minutes. Remove the herbs from the pan and refrigerate to cool. Chop the cooled herbs and purée with the remaining 2 tablespoons canola oil, the olive oil, and ice water until smooth. Strain through a fine-mesh sieve and season to taste with salt and pepper.

To prepare the vegetables: Sauté the carrots, Brussels sprouts, and zucchini in the butter over medium heat for 3 to 5 minutes, or until the vegetables are light golden brown. Add the water and cook for 5 minutes, or until the vegetables are tender. Season to taste with salt and pepper.

To prepare the catfish: Season the catfish with salt and pepper and sprinkle with the remaining 2 tablespoons chopped chives. Place on a wire rack in a steamer or in a sauté pan over simmering water. Cover with a lid and steam the catfish for 3 to 4 minutes, or until the catfish is completely cooked.

ASSEMBLY—Gently reheat the herb purée over medium-low heat. Spoon some of the white navy beans in the center of each plate and arrange the cooked carrots, Brussels sprouts, and zucchini over the beans. Place a piece of the catfish over the vegetables and spoon some of the herb purée around the plate.

WINE NOTES—The white navy beans in this dish add a richness and texture that pushes it toward a red wine. A delicate Pinot Noir like Robert Sinskey Vineyards is a perfect match.

TAMARI EGGDROP SOUP WITH SAUTÈED CATFISH AND BEAN THREAD NOODLES

This preparation is light and healthy,

but at the same time, it is very soothing and satisfying.

The toothsome noodles, crunchy vegetables, and silky broth offer

tremendous textural diversity,

and the catfish provides just the right amount of substance.

Any type of fish or shellfish could be used

in addition to or in place of the catfish for interesting variations.

SERVES 4

6 cups Chicken Stock (see page 201)

⅓ cup tamari soy sauce

1 teaspoon hoisin sauce

¼ cup minced fresh ginger

4 3-ounce pieces catfish

Salt and pepper

1 tablespoon canola oil

2 eggs, lightly beaten

4 ounces dried bean thread or cellophane noodles, cooked

½ cup enoki mushrooms

½ cup sliced water chestnuts

2 cups coarsely chopped bok choy, blanched

½ cup mung bean sprouts

2 tablespoons julienned nori

2 tablespoons radish sprouts

¼ cup sesame oil

METHOD—To make the soup: Place the stock, tamari, and hoisin sauce in a large saucepan and bring to a simmer. Add the ginger, simmer for 3 minutes, and remove from the heat.

To prepare the catfish: Season the catfish with salt and pepper. Place the canola oil in a hot sauté pan over medium heat, add the catfish, and cook for 2 minutes on each side, or until lightly golden brown.

ASSEMBLY—Bring the soup to a boil, quickly stir in the lightly beaten eggs, and remove from the heat. Place some of the bean thread noodles in the center of each bowl. Arrange some of the enoki mushrooms, water chestnuts, bok choy, and mung bean sprouts around the noodles. Place a piece of the catfish over the noodles and ladle in some of the hot tamari eggdrop soup. Sprinkle some of the julienned nori and radish sprouts around the bowl and drizzle some of the sesame oil in the soup.

WINE NOTES—Most Asian-style preparations blend beautifully with aromatic varietals. Try an Alsace Pinot Gris by producers like Domaine Weinbach or Trimbach. These light-bodied wines are refreshing and balance wonderfully with the elegant soup but still leave the delicate catfish in the spotlight.

CARAMELIZED ONION–CRUSTED CATFISH WITH SWEET CORN "RISOTTO"

Caramelized onions make an earthy yet elegant crust that shows off the refined flavor of catfish. The sating sweet corn "risotto" contains no arborio rice; instead, the corn is cooked like a risotto by adding liquid a little at a time and stirring continuously. The result is sensual but simple and straightforward. Lightly wilted lettuces add an important textural note that cuts into both the catfish and the sweet corn "risotto." For a more substantial meal, make a real risotto and simply add the corn just before serving.

SERVES 4

1 Spanish onion, minced

3 tablespoons butter

Salt and pepper

½ cup minced shallots

3 cups fresh sweet corn kernels

2 cups button mushrooms, diced

2 jalapeño peppers, sliced into thin rings

2 tablespoons Spicy Vinegar (see page 217)

¾ cup Chicken Stock (see page 201)

4 3-ounce pieces catfish

1 tablespoon canola oil

3 cups mesclun greens

METHOD—To prepare the caramelized onions: Sauté the onion in 1½ tablespoons of the butter over medium-high heat for 8 to 10 minutes, or until golden brown and caramelized. Season to taste with salt and pepper and keep warm.

To prepare the sweet corn "risotto": Sweat the shallots and remaining 1½ tablespoons butter in a large sauté pan over medium heat for 3 to 4 minutes, or until translucent. Add the corn, mushrooms, jalapeños, and Spicy Vinegar and cook over medium-low heat for 3 minutes. Add ¼ cup of the Chicken Stock and cook until most of the liquid is absorbed. Continue to add the Chicken Stock in ¼-cup additions until the corn mixture is cooked and all of the liquid is absorbed. Season to taste with salt and pepper.

To prepare the catfish: Season the catfish with salt and pepper and place in a hot sauté pan with the canola oil. Cook over medium-high heat for 2 to 3 minutes on each side, or until just cooked. Remove the catfish from the pan and add the mesclun to the pan. Quickly wilt the mesclun over medium heat for 1 minute and season to taste with salt and pepper.

ASSEMBLY—Spread a layer of the wilted greens in the center of each plate and top with some of the sweet corn "risotto." Completely cover the cooked catfish pieces with the caramelized onion and place a piece over the "risotto." Top with freshly ground black pepper.

WINE NOTES—The sweetness of the onion takes control in this preparation. The toasty oak of a Puligny-Montrachet by a producer such as Jean Marc Boillot is a wonderful balance to the caramelized flavor of the onion.

INDIAN CURRY–BRAISED CATFISH

As this dish slow-cooks, the spices bloom and develop a depth
that results in naturally complex flavors. The slightly overcooked fish has a buttery, meltaway texture,
and the chewy basmati rice perfectly balances the rich braising liquid. Best of all,
this preparation can be done in 30 minutes or less,
or even made ahead and heated up. Mushrooms can be added
if a little more substance or earthiness are desired.

SERVES 4

1 Spanish onion, julienned

1 tablespoon minced fresh ginger

1 tablespoon canola oil

1 Granny Smith apple,
peeled and diced

1 red bell pepper, julienned

½ teaspoon ground cumin

1 tablespoon sugar

½ teaspoon ground fenugreek

8 2-ounce pieces catfish

Salt and pepper

1 cup Apricot-Curry Sauce
(see page 198)

2 cups Chicken Stock (see page 201)

3 cups warm, cooked basmati rice

3 tablespoons chiffonade-cut
cilantro leaves

METHOD—To prepare the catfish: Caramelize the onion and ginger in a large saucepan in the canola oil for 5 minutes, or until golden brown. Add the apple, bell pepper, cumin, sugar, and fenugreek and cook for 5 minutes. Season the catfish pieces with salt and pepper and place over the vegetables. Add the Apricot-Curry Sauce and Chicken Stock and cover with a tight-fitting lid. Gently simmer the mixture for 8 to 12 minutes, or until the catfish pieces are almost falling apart.

ASSEMBLY—Place a mound of the warm basmati rice in the center of each shallow bowl. Arrange some of the catfish and vegetables over the rice and spoon some of the braising sauce from the pan over the catfish and around the bowl. Sprinkle with the cilantro and top with freshly ground black pepper.

WINE NOTES—The dominant curry flavors in this dish require the richness of a Napa or Monterey Chardonnay to keep them in balance. A full-bodied wine from producers such as Floral Springs or Talbott would be perfect.

Chapter

6

Salmon

POACHED SALMON WITH NOODLES, FENNEL, AND APPLE

Of all the fish and shellfish that can be poached,

salmon probably enjoys the easiest, most splendid results.

In this dish, the poaching liquid is used as the broth, which not only provides great flavor but it is also quite healthy.

The apple and fennel add pleasurable notes of

sweetness and texture

helping to make the final combination of flavors, aromas, and textures both

earthy and elegant. Any type or quantity of noodles can be used, or perhaps even rice,

making this dish easy to serve as an appetizer or an entrée.

SERVES 4

½ cup chopped carrots

½ cup chopped celery

½ cup chopped Spanish onion

½ cup chopped Granny Smith apple

½ cup chopped leeks

1 tablespoon black peppercorns

2 bay leaves

2 quarts water

⅓ cup fresh tarragon leaves

8 ounces dried fettuccini noodles, cooked and tossed with 2 tablespoons olive oil

1½ cups cremini mushrooms, cleaned and sliced

1 bulb fennel, julienned

4 4-ounce pieces salmon

Salt and pepper

1 Granny Smith apple, julienned

¼ cup coarsely chopped fennel tops

8 teaspoons olive oil

METHOD—To make the broth: Place the carrots, celery, onion, the chopped apple, leeks, black peppercorns, and bay leaves in a medium saucepan, cover with water, and simmer over medium heat for 30 minutes. Add the tarragon and continue to cook for 2 minutes. Strain the mixture through a fine-mesh sieve, return the broth to the saucepan, and bring to a simmer.

To reheat the noodles: Use a wide, shallow sieve to warm the noodles in the broth and then place them in a bowl.

To prepare the vegetables: Place the sliced mushrooms and julienned fennel in the broth, heat for 2 minutes, and remove from the broth.

To poach the salmon: Place the salmon in the broth and cook for 2 to 4 minutes, or until cooked medium. Remove the salmon and season with salt and pepper. Season the broth to taste with salt and pepper.

ASSEMBLY—Place some of the noodles, mushrooms, fennel, and julienned apple in the center of each bowl. Top with the salmon and ladle in some of the broth. Sprinkle some of the fennel tops around the bowl and drizzle some of the olive oil around the broth. Top with freshly ground black pepper.

WINE NOTES—A lean, crisp-style Sauvignon Blanc like Babcock "Eleven Oaks" from Santa Barbara will be perfect for this dish. The delicate citrus flavors play well with the salmon and apple, and the light fennel flavors of the Sauvignon Blanc really enhance those from the dish.

GRILLED SALMON STEAKS WITH ASPARAGUS AND SPICY EGGPLANT PURÉE

Salmon steaks are ½ to 1-inch-thick, cross-cut pieces of a whole salmon with the skin on and the main bones still intact. They are perfect for grilling because the strip of skin around the sides keeps the fish moist and juicy. Asparagus is a splendid accompaniment; it provides a textural contrast and the spears can be grilled right alongside of the fish. To keep this dish on the light and healthful side, I like to serve it with an eggplant purée sauce. Because the eggplant is thoroughly roasted before it is puréed, the flavor is wonderfully complex and utterly decadent while still being light.

SERVES 4

1 small eggplant, halved lengthwise

Salt and pepper

¾ cup plus 1 tablespoon olive oil

3 tablespoons Spicy Vinegar (see page 217)

¼ cup water

1 jalapeño, seeded and minced

3 tablespoons freshly squeezed lemon juice

¼ cup minced shallots

¼ cup chopped fresh tarragon

20 thin asparagus spears, cleaned and blanched

8 baby eggplants, halved

4 salmon steaks

¾ cup peeled, seeded, and diced tomato

4 tablespoons Tarragon Oil (see page 207, Herb Oil)

METHOD—To prepare the eggplant: Score the cut side of the eggplant, season with salt and pepper, and rub with 1 tablespoon of olive oil. Place the eggplant cut side down on a sheet pan. Fill the pan with ¼ inch of water and bake at 350 degrees for 30 minutes, or until the eggplant is tender. Purée the eggplant flesh with the Spicy Vinegar, water, jalapeño, and 2 tablespoons olive oil for 1 minute, or until smooth. Season to taste with salt and pepper.

To prepare the vegetables: Whisk together the remaining ½ cup plus 2 tablespoons of olive oil, the lemon juice, shallots, and tarragon in a small bowl and season to taste with salt and pepper. Toss the asparagus and baby eggplant with some of the tarragon mixture and heat on the grill for 2 minutes. Cut the asparagus in half lengthwise and cut the eggplant into thin strips.

To prepare the salmon: Brush the salmon lightly with some of the tarragon mixture and season with salt and pepper. Grill over a moderate flame for 2 to 3 minutes on each side, or until cooked medium-rare to medium.

ASSEMBLY—Warm the eggplant purée, spoon some in the center of each plate, and top with a salmon steak. Arrange the asparagus around the purée and sprinkle the eggplant strips and tomato around the asparagus. Spoon the remaining tarragon mixture over the salmon and asparagus, top with black pepper, and drizzle the Tarragon Oil around the plates.

WINE NOTES—Oak flavors are always a great match with anything grilled. Mount Adam from Australia is a great example and will also balance out the spice of the eggplant purée.

SMOKED SALMON CANAPÉS

The following are some of my favorite ways to serve smoked salmon.

In this recipe, I have assembled the canapés as a plated appetizer

but they could be served as individual, passed canapés. I think the

versatility of this fish is amply demonstrated with these preparations.

It can stand up to assertive Asian flavors or act as the backdrop to something

luxurious like caviar.

If you want to achieve a slightly different flavor, smoked sturgeon could be substituted

in any of these recipes with equally fabulous results.

SERVES 8

½ cup crème fraîche

2 tablespoons water

Salt and pepper

1 ounce caviar

Smoked Salmon Terrine
(recipe follows)

1 cup baby cress
(or other tiny lettuce or sprouts)

8 teaspoons olive oil (optional)

Smoked Salmon and Avocado
Maki Rolls (recipe follows)

Smoked Salmon Tartar on Brioche
(recipe follows)

Smoked Salmon Rolls with Hot and
Sour Cucumbers (recipe follows)

METHOD—To prepare the caviar–crème fraîche: Place the crème fraîche and water in a small bowl, whisk together until smooth, and season to taste with pepper. Gently fold in the caviar. Use immediately; if the mixture stands too long, the caviar breaks down and the crème fraîche turns gray.

ASSEMBLY—Place a triangle of the salmon terrine upright on one corner of each plate and spoon some of the caviar–crème fraîche around it. Sprinkle some of the baby cress around the terrine. Drizzle the terrine with a teaspoon of olive oil if a richer presentation is desired. Place a Smoked Salmon and Avocado Maki Roll on the opposite corner. Place a Smoked Salmon Tartar on Brioche and a Smoked Salmon Roll with Hot and Sour Cucumbers on the remaining corners of the plate.

WINE NOTES—Canapés are always best with Champagne. Crisp styles like Veuve Clicquot and Pol Roger are perfect, or for a very special occasion, try a vintage Krug. If you prefer a nonsparkling wine, a Sancerre will be a great match for the rich salmon.

Smoked Salmon Rolls with Hot and Sour Cucumbers

Assemble these rolls just prior to serving or the pickling juice will cook the salmon.

YIELD: 8 ROLLS

1 cup Hot and Sour Cucumbers (see page 207)

8 thin slices smoked salmon

METHOD—To prepare the salmon rolls: Drain any liquid from the cucumbers. Lay the salmon slices on a work surface and place some of the hot and sour cucumbers in the middle of one of the slices. Roll up the salmon slice from one end to the other, keeping the cucumbers securely inside. Repeat with the remaining slices of salmon and cucumbers.

Smoked Salmon and Avocado Maki Roll

You can easily substitute any other fish or vegetables for the salmon and avocado in these maki rolls.

YIELD: 8 PIECES

$1\frac{1}{2}$ cups cooked sushi rice, cooled

2 tablespoons rice wine vinegar

$1\frac{1}{2}$ tablespoons sugar

2 teaspoons wasabi powder

1 teaspoon water

2 sheets nori

6 long chives

4 8-inch-long by $\frac{1}{4}$-inch-wide strips smoked salmon

$\frac{1}{2}$ avocado, peeled and cut into batons

2 tablespoons wasabi tobiko

METHOD—To prepare the maki rolls: Place the rice in a medium bowl, add the vinegar and sugar, and mix until thoroughly combined. Place the wasabi and water in a small cup and stir until smooth. Lay a sheet of nori flat on a bamboo maki roller. Place $\frac{1}{2}$ cup of the rice on top of the nori. (Moisten your hands with water before touching the rice to prevent the rice from sticking to your hands.) Spread the rice flat, leaving a 2-inch border at the top of the nori. Spread some of the wasabi mixture on top of the rice and lay 3 of the chives horizontally in the center of the rice. Lay 2 strips of the smoked salmon and some of the avocado over the chives. Using the maki roller, carefully roll up the nori sheet, creating a firm, smooth maki roll. Moisten the 2-inch border of the nori with water and press against the roll to create a seal. Set the maki roll aside and repeat the process. Trim the ends of each maki roll, slice in half, then slice each of the 4 pieces in half on the diagonal. Spoon some of the wasabi tabiko over each maki roll piece just prior to serving.

Smoked Salmon Terrine

This terrine can be made the day ahead

and then sliced just prior to serving.

YIELD: 1 TERRINE (8 INCHES LONG BY 1½ INCHES WIDE BY 2¼ INCHES HIGH)

¼ cup butter, at room temperature

1 shallot, finely minced

1 tablespoon freshly squeezed lemon juice

1 tablespoon lemon zest, finely chopped

Black pepper

1½ pounds thinly sliced smoked salmon, cut into 1½-inch-wide strips

METHOD—To prepare the lemon butter: Place the butter, shallot, lemon juice, and lemon zest in a small bowl. Mix until smooth and season with pepper.

To prepare the terrine: Line an 8-inch long by 1½-inch wide by 2¼-inch high terrine mold with plastic wrap. Place a layer of the smoked salmon on the bottom of the mold and spread with a very thin layer of the lemon butter. Continue to layer the salmon and butter until all of the salmon is used. Cover the terrine with plastic wrap and refrigerate for at least 2 hours. Leaving the plastic wrap on, slice the terrine into ½-inch-thick slices. Carefully remove the plastic wrap and cut each slice in half on the diagonal.

Smoked Salmon Tartar on Brioche

The brioche can be toasted earlier in the day but the capers

should not be added

to the tartar until you are ready to use it.

YIELD: 8 PIECES

½ cup finely diced smoked salmon

2 tablespoons chopped fresh chervil

1 tablespoon chopped capers

1 tablespoon chopped shallots

2 teaspoons olive oil

Black pepper

8 thin 1-inch squares toasted Brioche (see page 201)

METHOD—To prepare the salmon: Place the smoked salmon, chervil, capers, shallots, and olive oil in a small bowl and mix thoroughly. Season to taste with the freshly ground black pepper. Place some of the smoked salmon tartar on each piece of toasted Brioche (or any type of crouton) just prior to serving.

SLOW–ROASTED SALMON WITH RED MISO— LEMONGRASS BROTH

The technique of very slowly cooking salmon results in some of the

most succulent fish I have ever tasted. Any fish with a high fat content, like salmon, can be roasted at a very low

temperature on a bed of vegetables with fairly stunning results.

Not only is the flavor of the fish enhanced by the vegetables, but

the texture is utterly sublime.

In this dish, the red miso adds a haunting elegance, and the lemongrass provides just the right sharpness.

Also, much of the work for this dish can be done while the fish is cooking.

SERVES 4

2 cups Chicken Stock (see page 201)

4 tablespoons butter

1 large turnip, peeled and cut into batons

Salt and pepper

¼ cup chopped lemongrass

1 cup 1-inch-thick leek slices (white part only)

1 tablespoon rice wine vinegar

1 tablespoon tamari soy sauce

1 tablespoon red miso

4 4-ounce pieces salmon

2 tablespoons olive oil

3 cups watercress, thick stems removed

METHOD—To prepare the broth: Place the Chicken Stock, 2 tablespoons of the butter, and the turnip in a medium saucepan and bring to a simmer. Cook for 3 to 4 minutes, or until the turnip is about half cooked. Remove the turnips from the liquid and season to taste with salt and pepper. Add the lemongrass to the liquid, simmer for 7 minutes, strain, and discard the lemongrass. Add the leek to the liquid and cook for 7 minutes, or until the leeks are soft. Add the rice wine vinegar, tamari, and red miso and cook for 2 minutes. Season to taste with salt and pepper.

To prepare the salmon: Season the salmon with salt and pepper and rub with the olive oil. Place the turnip batons on a sheet pan and place the salmon on top. Roast in the oven at 250 degrees for 15 to 20 minutes, or until the salmon is cooked medium.

To prepare the watercress: Wilt the watercress in a hot sauté pan with 2 tablespoons of butter for 2 minutes and season to taste with salt and pepper.

ASSEMBLY—Reheat the broth, if necessary. Place some of the wilted watercress and turnip batons in the center of each shallow bowl and top with a piece of the salmon. Ladle some of the warm broth in the bowls and over the salmon. Top with freshly ground black pepper.

WINE NOTES—An Austrian Riesling is a great match for the red miso-lemongrass broth. The full-bodied, dry, and intensely aromatic style by producers like Prager and Knoll are a wonderful complement to the haunting flavors in this dish. For the perfect pairing, try a Prager "Steinriegl" Federspiel Riesling.

SAUTÉED SALMON WITH ONION–STREWN GRITS AND PORTOBELLO MUSHROOM—RED WINE SAUCE

Leaving the skin on the salmon creates

a crispy, crackly layer that melts into the flesh with each bite.

A buttery, sweet mound

of grits with caramelized red onion makes for a hearty, yet subtle textural contrast.

And to further push this preparation into soul-satisfying territory, it is paired with an earthy, yet refined,

Portobello Mushroom-Red Wine Sauce. Other seafood items could easily replace the salmon here,

and the resulting flavors and textures would satisfy

even the most avid meat lover.

SERVES 4

1 red onion, julienned

3 tablespoons butter

3 tablespoons chopped chives

2½ tablespoons lemon juice

2 cups cooked white grits

Salt and pepper

2 Roasted Portobello Mushroom (see page 214)

½ cup Red Wine Jus (see page 213)

¼ cup olive oil

1 teaspoon chopped shallot

4 4-ounce pieces salmon, skin on and scored with a razor blade

2 tablespoons canola oil

1 tablespoon 1-inch-long chive pieces

METHOD—To prepare the grits: Cook the onion in a hot sauté pan with 1 table-spoon of the butter for 5 to 8 minutes, or until golden brown and caramelized. Fold the onion, 2 tablespoons of chives, and 1 tablespoon of lemon juice into the grits and season with salt and pepper.

To prepare the sauce: Coarsely chop 1 of the mushrooms, place in the blender with the Red Wine Jus, and purée for 2 minutes, or until smooth. Place the mushroom purée in a small saucepan and warm over medium heat. Whisk in the remaining 2 tablespoons butter and season to taste with salt and pepper.

To prepare the vinaigrette: Whisk together the olive oil, 1 tablespoon chopped chives, 1½ tablespoons lemon juice, and shallots. Season with salt and pepper.

To prepare the salmon: Season the salmon with salt and pepper. Place, skin side down, in a hot sauté pan with the canola oil and cook for 2 to 3 minutes on each side, or until golden brown and cooked medium.

ASSEMBLY—Thinly slice the portobello mushroom. Place a small mound of the grits in the center of each plate and top with the mushrooms. Place a piece of the salmon on the mushrooms and spoon the portobello mushroom—red wine sauce around the plate. Spoon the vinaigrette on the fish and around the plates and sprinkle with the chive pieces. Top with black pepper.

WINE NOTES—An earthy, aromatic red Burgundy will bring this dish to another level. Vosne-Romanee by producers such as Mongeard-Mugneret or Jean Gros will heighten the flavors of the carmelized onion and mushroom, but still allow the rich salmon to shine through.

SALAD OF DARJEELING TEA—CURED SALMON WITH CITRUS—GINGER—ALMOND VINAIGRETTE

It's actually quite simple to cure salmon.

All that you need is a small quantity of salt, sugar, and flavoring components.

Citrus, peppercorns, herbs, or ginger are all great options, but this version features the surprisingly elegant flavor of Darjeeling tea.

The tea has a very clean flavor, with just a hint of smokiness that makes it especially interesting.

Combined with salad greens, a little pear or apple, and the aromatic, refreshing vinaigrette, this salad has extraordinary depth and can work as a light, small course, or as a more substantial appetizer.

SERVES 4

2 bay leaves, crushed

2 tablespoons black peppercorns

2 cloves

1 small dried chile, chopped

3 allspice berries

1 tablespoon orange zest

½ tablespoon lemon zest

1 teaspoon lime zest

½ cup dried Darjeeling tea

3 ounces vodka

3 cups sugar

3 cups kosher salt

1½-pound salmon fillet

½ cup almond slivers, toasted

½ cup freshly squeezed orange juice

1 tablespoon minced ginger

¾ cup olive oil

1 tablespoon rice wine vinegar

Salt and pepper

4 cups mesclun greens

1 pear, peeled, cored, and sliced

½ cup thinly sliced radishes

1 cup thinly sliced button mushrooms

METHOD—To prepare the salmon: Cook the bay leaves, peppercorns, cloves, chile, and allspice in a medium sauté pan for 2 to 3 minutes, or until the spices become aromatic. Add the orange, lemon, and lime zest and the Darjeeling tea and cook for 1 minute. Remove from the heat and add the vodka. Place the mixture in a large bowl, add the sugar and salt, and stir until well combined. Pour half of the mixture onto a baking sheet and place the salmon fillet on top. Completely cover any exposed salmon with the remaining cure. Place in the refrigerator for 24 to 36 hours depending on the thickness of the fillet.

Rinse the cure from the salmon and let sit uncovered in the refrigerator for an additional 24 hours to develop the pellicle (a dry outer layer of the flesh). Once the pellicle has developed, the salmon is ready to slice.

To prepare the vinaigrette: Purée 5 tablespoons of almonds with the orange juice and ginger and strain through a fine-mesh sieve. Whisk the mixture with the olive oil and rice wine vinegar and season to taste with salt and pepper.

To prepare the salad: Place the mesclun, pear slices, radish slices, mushrooms, and remaining 3 tablespoons of almonds in a mixing bowl. Toss with about half of the vinaigrette and season to taste with salt and pepper.

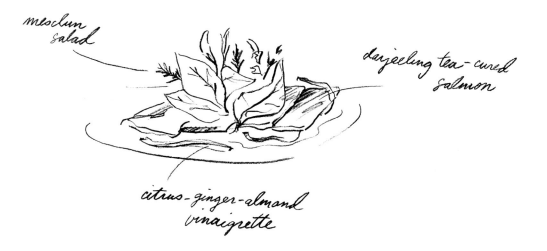

mesclun salad

darjeeling tea-cured salmon

citrus-ginger-almond vinaigrette

ASSEMBLY—Using a very sharp knife, cut the salmon into paper-thin slices. Place a few slices of the cured salmon in the center of each plate and top with a mound of the salad. Spoon some of the remaining vinaigrette around the plate and top with freshly ground black pepper.

WINE NOTES—Sancerre is usually the wine of choice with smoked salmon yet, with the tea influence, a more herbaceaous style of Sauvignon Blanc is a better choice. The racey acidity and delicate herbal flavors of Rochioli Sauvignon Blanc make it a perfect companion to this cured salmon.

Chapter 7

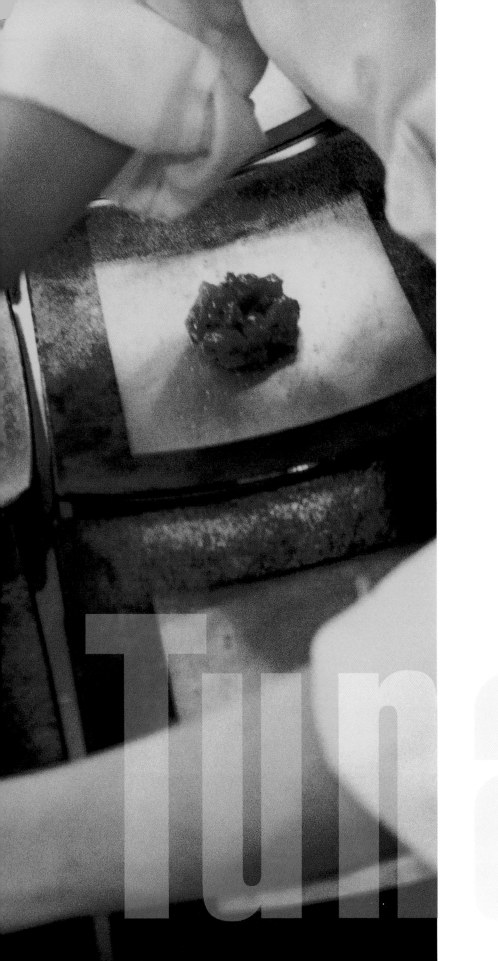

Tuna

CUMIN-CRUSTED TUNA LOIN WITH WILD MUSHROOM-STREWN BARLEY AND RED WINE EMULSION

Cumin is a great spice to pair with tuna

because it has a strong enough flavor to stand up to

the richness of the fish without being overwhelming.

The earthy mushroom-strewn barley enhances the exotic flavor of the cumin in this dish,

while the red wine emulsion provides a fruity acid that cuts the richness of the tuna

and barley. The addition of the satiny red wine emulsion

elevates this semihearty dish to a decidedly elegant plane.

SERVES 4

½ cup small-diced carrots

½ cup small-diced celery

½ cup small-diced onions

2 tablespoons canola oil

1 bay leaf

1 cup pearl barley

3¼ cups Chicken Stock, hot
(see page 201)

2 tablespoons coarsely chopped
marjoram leaves

2 cups Roasted Chanterelle
Mushrooms, quartered
(see page 214)

1 tablespoon lemon juice

Salt and pepper

4 3-ounce pieces tuna loin

2 tablespoons cumin seeds, toasted
and coarsely ground

1 cup Red Wine Jus (see page 213)

3 tablespoons butter

4 teaspoons chervil leaves

4 teaspoons marjoram leaves

METHOD—To prepare the barley: Cook the carrots, celery, and onions in a medium saucepan over medium-high heat with 1 tablespoon of the canola oil for 5 minutes, or until golden brown and caramelized. Add the bay leaf and barley. Add ½ cup of the Chicken Stock and cook over medium-low heat, stirring continuously. Continue to add the stock in ½-cup additions until 3 cups of stock have been used and the barley is tender. Fold in the marjoram leaves, mushrooms, and lemon juice and season with salt and pepper.

To prepare the tuna: Season the outside of the tuna with salt and pepper and coat with the ground cumin. Place the remaining 1 tablespoon of canola oil in a hot sauté pan and quickly sear each side of the tuna for 1 minute, or until golden brown. Slice each piece on the bias and season the inside flesh with salt and pepper.

To prepare the emulsion: Place the Red Wine Jus and the remaining ¼ cup stock in a small saucepan and warm over medium heat. Using a handheld blender, whip in the butter and blend until frothy. Season to taste with salt and pepper.

ASSEMBLY—Spoon some of the warm barley mixture in the center of each plate and top with 2 slices of tuna. Spoon the Red Wine Emulsion around the plate and sprinkle with the chervil and marjoram leaves.

WINE NOTES—Grenache-based wines have enough acidity and spice to perfectly balance the cumin and mushrooms in the dish. The Châteauneuf-du-Pape-style wine Le Cigar Volante by Bonny Doon Vineyards enhances this dish wonderfully.

BASIL OIL—MARINATED TUNA WITH DAIKON SALAD AND MEYER LEMON

When you are able to buy pristine sashimi grade tuna, it's best to enjoy it simply prepared; thinly sliced with a little soy sauce or with just the slightest flavor and textural enhancements. In this case, Basil Oil adds a bit of delightful opulence, although plain olive oil also works just fine. Droplets of something not overly acidic, like Meyer lemon or orange juice, provide the **perfect counterbalance** to the fat in the fish and the oil. And a crunchy element, like daikon, jicama, or even celery, acts as the ultimate exclamation point, keeping the simple flavors exciting and fresh bite after bite.

SERVES 4

2 Meyer lemons

1 cup finely julienned daikon

2 tablespoons basil chiffonade

Salt and pepper

12 ounces tuna, cut into 36 very thin slices (about 1 by 1½ inches)

¼ cup Basil Oil (see page 198)

METHOD—To prepare the lemon fillets: Cut the peel and bitter white pith off the lemons and slice along each side of the membranes to remove the fillets. Discard the membranes, reserving any juice.

To prepare the daikon salad: Place the daikon in a small bowl and toss with the basil and 2 teaspoons of the reserved lemon juice. Season to taste with salt and pepper.

To prepare the tuna: Lay the tuna slices on a plate and brush with some of the Basil Oil. Season each slice with salt and pepper.

ASSEMBLY—Lay 9 slices of tuna in the center of each plate and place a small mound of the daikon salad in the center of the tuna. Arrange a few of the lemon fillets over the tuna slices and spoon a few teaspoons of the Basil Oil around the plate. Top with freshly ground black pepper and spoon some of the remaining lemon juice over the tuna slices.

WINE NOTES—The delicate citrus notes and vibrant acidity in the Rieslings from South Australia will balance well with this preparation. The innovative style of producers like Grosset and Pikes makes a marvelous example of this grape.

GRILLED TUNA STEAKS WITH SPICY LENTIL VINAIGRETTE AND CURRY OIL

Tuna right off the grill is a glorious treat, but only if it's treated like a strip steak and cooked rare to medium-rare. Here, braised lentils provide a chewy earthiness that is just the right foil to the succulent tuna A drizzle of Curry Oil provides an exotic flavor that verges on the poetic. Any legume could be substituted for the lentils with fabulous results, and if curry is not your flavor of choice, try an herbed citrus vinaigrette instead. You'll be amazed at the overall depth of flavor.

SERVES 4

¼ cup brunoise-cut carrots

¼ cup brunoise-cut celery

¼ cup finely diced onion

2 teaspoons peeled, minced fresh ginger

1 tablespoon canola oil

¼ cup peeled, brunoise-cut Granny Smith apple

½ cup French green lentils

1½ cups water, or more, as needed

4 tablespoons Spicy Vinegar (see page 217)

½ cup olive oil

Salt and pepper

4 5-ounce tuna steaks

Curry Oil (see page 202)

4 cups shredded napa cabbage

2 tablespoons butter

METHOD—To prepare the lentils: Cook the carrots, celery, onion, and ginger in the canola oil in a medium saucepan over medium heat for 5 minutes, or until lightly caramelized. Add the apple and lentils and cook for 1 minute. Add the water and bring to a slow simmer. Continue to cook over low heat, stirring occasionally, for 1 hour, or until all the liquid has been absorbed and the lentils are tender. If the water has been absorbed and the lentils are not tender, add additional water, several tablespoons at a time, until the lentils are completely cooked. Add 3 tablespoons Spicy Vinegar and the olive oil and season to taste with salt and pepper.

To prepare the tuna: Season the tuna steaks with salt and pepper and brush with a light coating of the Curry Oil. Grill the tuna steaks over a moderate flame for 2 to 3 minutes on each side, or until the tuna is cooked medium-rare.

To prepare the cabbage: Place the napa cabbage in a sauté pan over medium heat and quickly wilt with the butter and the remaining 1 tablespoon Spicy Vinegar. Season to taste with salt and pepper.

ASSEMBLY—Place some of the wilted napa cabbage in the center of each plate and top with a piece of tuna. Spoon the lentil vinaigrette over the tuna and around the plate and drizzle 2 teaspoons of the Curry Oil around the lentils.

WINE NOTES—The Curry Oil in the dish adds a delicate spice that needs the richness of Chardonnay to completely cleanse. Chalk Hill "Estate Vineyard Selection" Chardonnay has just enough richness and vibrant acidity to balance the oil and showcase the tuna.

102

WARM TUNA SALAD WITH OLIVE OIL–POACHED TOMATOES, HARICOTS VERTS, NEW POTATOES, AND BLACK OLIVE–CAPER VINAIGRETTE

This lusty dish is a variation on a classic salad niçoise. The olive oil–poached tomatoes melt like butter, but maintain just enough meatiness to provide a satisfactory texture. The new potatoes add substance, and the haricots verts supply not only a great cleansing quality, but a fabulous crunchy texture as well. The vinaigrette is earthy and sensual and definitely ties these disparate flavors and textures together. You can substitute chicken, pork, steak, or even salmon for the tuna.

SERVES 4

4 4-ounce pieces tuna

Salt and pepper

2 tablespoons canola oil

4 cups baby spinach, cleaned

1½ cups haricots verts, blanched

12 tiny new potatoes, boiled and quartered

½ cup julienned prosciutto

1 cup Olive Oil–Poached Tomatoes (see page 210)

Black Olive–Caper Vinaigrette (see page 200)

1 hard-boiled egg white, passed through a sieve

METHOD—To prepare the tuna: Season the tuna with salt and pepper and place in a hot sauté pan with the canola oil. Cook for 2 to 3 minutes on each side, or until cooked medium-rare. Remove tuna from the pan.

To prepare the vegetables: Place the spinach in the pan from the tuna and remove from the heat. Quickly toss for 30 seconds, or until the spinach is just barely wilted. Place the spinich, haricots verts, potatoes, prosciutto, remaining olives, and the tomatoes in a large bowl and toss with half of the Black Olive–Caper Vinaigrette. Season to taste with salt and pepper.

ASSEMBLY—Thinly slice the tuna. Place some of the spinach mixture in the center of each plate and top with some of the tuna slices. Sprinkle the plate with the egg white and spoon the remaining vinaigrette over the tuna and around the plate.

WINE NOTES—The warm flavors from the tomatoes and vinaigrette are complemented by the floral earthiness of Bandol Rosé by Domaine Tempier. The Provencal influences in this dish make it a perfect companion to this wine from Provence.

SEARED TUNA WITH FENNEL BROTH,
HERBED SPAETZLE, AND SUNDRIED TOMATOES

This light, fragrant fennel broth is incredibly soothing

and beautifully showcases the clean, rich flavor of the seared tuna. You could also use a full-flavored vegetable

broth or a light chicken broth with equally majestic results.

The slightly chewy spaetzel in this dish provides a deeply satisfying textural note, and

the sun-dried tomatoes add a sweet earthiness.

By increasing the portion size and adding some roasted vegetables,

this dish could easily become a meal in itself.

SERVES 4

1 egg, beaten

2 tablespoons chopped parsley

1 cup flour

½ cup milk

Salt and pepper

6 cups fennel juice (about 10 bulbs)

2 cups julienned fennel

3 tablespoons canola oil

12 ounces tuna loin

¼ cup sundried tomatoes, julienned

4 teaspoons olive oil

4 teaspoons coarsely chopped fennel tops

METHOD—To prepare the spaetzle: Combine the egg, parsley, and flour. Add enough milk to make a somewhat stiff batter. Cover and refrigerate for 1 hour.

Using a pastry bag or spaetzle maker, drop ¼ teaspoonfuls of batter into simmering, lightly salted water. Cook for 1 minute, or until the spaetzle floats. Drain the spaetzle and season to taste with salt and pepper. (Toss the spaetzle with a little olive oil if you are not using it immediately.)

To prepare the broth: Bring the fennel juice to a simmer and cook for 5 minutes. Strain the juice through a fine-mesh sieve lined with cheesecloth or a coffee filter and season to taste with salt and pepper.

To prepare the fennel: Sauté the julienned fennel in 1 tablespoon of the canola oil for 5 minutes, or until golden brown, and season with salt and pepper.

To make the tuna: Season the tuna with salt and pepper and place in a very hot sauté pan with the remaining 2 tablespoons of canola oil. Quickly sear the tuna on each side and remove from the pan, leaving the tuna rare inside. Slice the tuna into 20 thin slices and season to taste with salt and pepper.

ASSEMBLY—Place some of the sundried tomatoes, julienned fennel, and spaetzle in the center of each bowl. Arrange 5 of the tuna slices over the spaetzle and ladle in some of the fennel broth. Drizzle the olive oil around each bowl and sprinkle with the fennel tops. Top with freshly ground black pepper.

WINE NOTES—The delicate fennel and caraway flavors in Cloudy Bay Sauvignon Blanc from New Zealand echo those in the broth. The wine also has ripe citrus flavors, which are a wonderful complement to the tuna.

TUNA "NAPOLEON" WITH CRISPY POTATO TUILES AND CUCUMBER–YOGURT SAUCE

A dish like this is whimsical, fun to serve, and even more fun to eat. Plus, your guests will be amazed at your technical prowess when they see this stunning presentation, and you will be surprised at how simple it is to make. When you take a bite of this layered creation you experience several tremendous flavors and textural sensations simultaneously. The satiny tuna, lush mango, creamy avocado, crunchy potato tuiles and the cleansing cucumber-yogurt sauce all blend together superbly. Sometimes I make the yogurt sauce extra spicy by adding more chiles or perhaps a touch of chile vinegar.

SERVES 4

½ cup thinly sliced mango

Pickling Juice (see page 211)

1 medium avocado, peeled and pitted

1 tablespoon freshly squeezed lime juice

Dash of hot sauce

1 tablespoon minced shallot

Salt and pepper

½ cup Hot and Sour Cucumbers, plus 3 tablespoons liquid (see page 207)

½ cup plain yogurt

1 jalapeño pepper, seeded and minced

1 tablespoon chopped fresh dill

6 ounces tuna, cut into 16 thin slices

Dill Oil (see page 203)

12 Crispy Potato Tuiles (recipe follows)

METHOD—To prepare the mango: Place the mango slices and the Pickling Juice in a medium bowl and marinate for 1 hour at room temperature. Drain the mango from the Pickling Juice just prior to use.

To prepare the avocado: Mash together the avocado, lime juice, hot sauce, and shallot with a fork until smooth. Season to taste with salt and pepper.

To prepare the cucumber-yogurt sauce: Finely chop ¼ cup Hot and Sour Cucumbers. Place the chopped cucumbers, yogurt, jalapeño, and the cucumber liquid in a small bowl and mix well. Add the dill and season to taste with salt and pepper.

To prepare the tuna: Brush the tuna slices lightly with some of the Dill Oil and season with salt and pepper.

crispy potato tuiles

hot & sour cucumbers

tuna

ASSEMBLY—Place 1 slice of the tuna in the center of each plate and top with a few slices of the mango and a few slices of Hot and Sour Cucumbers. Place a dollop of the avocado mixture on the cucumbers and place a Crispy Potato Tuile on top. Repeat this process until you have 4 layers of tuna and 3 layers of Crispy Potato Tuiles. Spoon some of the cucumber-yogurt sauce and drizzle 2 teaspoons of the Dill Oil around the plate.

WINE NOTES—The flavors of this wonderfully delicate tuna should not be hidden by a heavy wine, but the mango adds a richness that needs a substantial wine. The Blancs de Blanc sparkling wine from Schramsberg Vineyard has a beautifully cleansing effervescence and enough richness to handle the mango.

Crispy Potato Tuiles

This recipe yields extra tuiles in case of breakage or for snacking.

YIELD: ABOUT 40 TUILES OR 1 CUP OF BATTER

1 Idaho potato (about 10 ounces), baked and riced

2 tablespoons butter

4 egg whites

Salt and pepper

METHOD—Place the warm, riced potatoes in a mixing bowl with the butter and egg whites and mix with an electric mixer on medium speed until smooth. Season to taste with salt and pepper. Pass the mixture through a sieve to remove any lumps. Spread a very thin layer of the potato batter into 2-inch-circles on a nonstick sheet pan. Repeat this process until you have at least 12 tuiles. Bake at 350 degrees for 10 to 15 minutes, or until the tuiles are golden brown. Carefully remove the tuiles from the sheet pan and set aside to cool. Store in an airtight container at room temperature for up to 1 day.

Chapter

8

Pasta

BUFFALO MILK MOZZARELLA LASAGNA WITH OVEN-DRIED YELLOW TOMATOES AND ROASTED RED BELL PEPPER SAUCE

Buffalo milk mozzarella and oven-dried tomatoes make this vegetarian lasagna especially unique.

Plus there is no limit to the ingredients

that can be added to the filling to suit your tastes; mushrooms, chiles, ground shrimp, ground lamb—

practically anything—works wonderfully.

Once you go through the exercise of assembling and baking the lasagna,

and taste the brilliant results, you will be compelled to experiment.

Ideally, this lasagna should be made a day or two ahead of time to

allow all the flavors to meld together.

SERVES 10

6 yellow tomatoes

6 red tomatoes

Salt and pepper

1 cup chopped fresh basil leaves

½ cup olive oil

3 Roasted Red Bell Peppers
(see page 213)

Semolina Pasta (see page 215)

1 large red onion, sliced

1½ cups ricotta cheese

2 tablespoons chopped
fresh parsley leaves

1½ pounds buffalo milk mozzarella

3 Roasted Yellow Bell Peppers
(see page 213)

2 tablespoons minced garlic

¾ pound mozzarella cheese, grated

2 yellow squash, thinly sliced

2 zucchini, thinly sliced

4 teaspoons tiny basil leaves

4 teaspoons Basil Oil (see page 198)

METHOD—To prepare oven-dried tomatoes: Cut the yellow and red tomatoes into ½-inch thick slices. Lay the tomato slices on sheet pans lined with wire racks. Season the tomatoes with salt and pepper, sprinkle with ½ cup of the basil, and lightly drizzle with 3 tablespoons of the olive oil. Bake the tomatoes at 300 degrees for 2 hours, or until the tomato slices are dry to the touch but still moist inside. Remove from the oven and let cool to room temperature.

To prepare the bell pepper sauce: Peel, seed, and derib the Roasted Red Bell Peppers. Purée the peppers and 3 tablespoons of the olive oil until smooth and pass the purée through a fine-mesh sieve. Cook over medium heat for 5 minutes, or until warm. Season to taste with salt and pepper.

To prepare the yellow tomato sauce: Purée the oven-dried yellow tomato slices until smooth and pass through a fine-mesh sieve. Cook over medium heat for 5 minutes, or until warm. Season to taste with salt and pepper.

To prepare the pasta: Roll the Semolina Pasta out to 1/16-inch thick and cut into 2 by 8-inch strips. Cook the pasta in boiling salted water for 2 to 3 minutes, or until al dente. Drain and trim the strips to fit the length of an 8 by 8-inch ovenproof lasagna pan. Lay the strips flat on a lightly oiled sheet pan until ready to use.

To prepare the caramelized onions: Sauté the red onion with the remaining 2 tablespoons olive oil over medium heat for 7 to 9 minutes, or until golden brown. Let cool to room temperature.

To prepare the ricotta: Combine the ricotta, parsley, and 6 tablespoons of the basil in a small bowl.

To assemble the lasagna: Cut the buffalo milk mozzarella into ¼-inch thick slices. Peel, seed, and derib the Roasted Yellow Bell Peppers. Lightly oil the bottom of the lasagna pan and sprinkle with the minced garlic. Cover the bottom of the pan with a layer of the cooked pasta strips. Spread a thin layer of the ricotta mixture over the pasta. Layer the ingredients, adding the oven-dried red tomatoes, followed by the grated mozzarella, yellow squash, caramelized red onions, buffalo mozzarella, pasta, ricotta, roasted yellow bell pepper, grated mozzarella, and zucchini. Add another layer of pasta and ricotta and end with a layer of buffalo mozzarella. Bake the lasagna at 350 degrees for 60 to 90 minutes, or until light golden brown. Allow the lasagna to rest for 20 minutes before slicing.

ASSEMBLY—Spoon a wide circle of the yellow tomato sauce in the center of each plate. Place a piece of the lasagna in the center of the plate and spoon some of the roasted red bell pepper sauce around the lasagna. Sprinkle with the tiny basil leaves and drizzle the Basil Oil around the plates. Top with freshly ground black pepper.

WINE NOTES—A full-bodied Chardonnay such as Scotchman's Hill from Victoria, Australia, blends wonderfully with the delicate richness of the buffalo mozzarella. And the acidity of the wine seems to cut through the sweetness of the bell pepper and tomato, making this a perfect match.

NOODLE GALETTES WITH SAUTÉED MUSHROOMS
AND CUMIN-INFUSED CELERY ROOT BROTH

This dish is lovely for a special dinner, and it's much easier to prepare than it looks. Sautéing the galette in a little butter slightly browns and crisps the edges while leaving the noodles inside satisfyingly chewy. Sautéed mushrooms and lettuce provide earthiness and a delicate crunchiness respectively to complement the crispy noodles. Everything swims in a full-flavored but light cumin-infused celery root broth. The resulting flavor and texture combination is utterly haunting. For more substance, a piece of chicken or fish can be placed right on top of the noodles.

SERVES 4

8 ounces capellini

Salt and pepper

2 tablespoons butter

1 shallot, minced

1 cup oyster mushrooms

1 cup hedgehog mushrooms

1 head Boston lettuce, coarsely chopped

2 tablespoons verjuice

6 cups celery root juice

1 tablespoon cumin seeds, toasted and ground

¼ cup celery leaves

2 tablespoons chiffonade-cut red swiss chard

4 teaspoons olive oil

METHOD—To prepare the galette: Cook the capellini in boiling salted water for 5 to 7 minutes, or until al dente. Drain and season with salt and pepper. Line an 8 by 8-inch pan with plastic wrap and spread the warm capellini evenly in the pan. Cover tightly with plastic wrap, place another 8 by 8-inch pan on top of the capellini, and weight it down with a brick or other heavy, ovenproof object. Refrigerate for at least 3 hours.

Remove the weighted pan and the top layer of plastic wrap from the galette. Using a 2½-inch ring cutter, cut 4 discs out of the noodle galette. Place 1 tablespoon of the butter in a hot, nonstick sauté pan and quickly add the 4 galettes. Cook over high heat for 2 to 3 minutes on each side, or until golden brown and crispy. Remove the galettes from the pan and blot on paper towels.

To prepare the mushrooms and lettuce: Place the shallot and remaining 1 tablespoon butter in a hot sauté pan and cook for 1 minute. Add the oyster and hedgehog mushrooms and cook for 3 to 4 minutes, or until the mushrooms are tender. Add the Boston lettuce and verjuice, and cook for 2 to 3 minutes, or until the lettuce is wilted. Season to taste with salt and pepper.

To prepare the broth: Simmer the celery root juice and cumin over medium heat for 10 minutes and strain through a fine-mesh sieve. Season to taste with salt and pepper.

ASSEMBLY—Place some of the mushroom and lettuce mixture in the center of each shallow bowl and top with a warm galette. Ladle some of the celery root broth into the bowls and sprinkle with the celery leaves and swiss chard. Drizzle the olive oil around the plates and top with freshly ground black pepper.

WINE NOTES—Celery root is the dominant flavor of this dish. The lean and aromatic style of a Gavi from Italy is a refreshing companion to this delicate broth and allows the flavors of the mushroom to shine through. A producer such as Massone, with its delicate acidity and floral aromatics, is perfect.

SALAD OF FUSILLI AND SMOKED CHICKEN
WITH ANCHOVY VINAIGRETTE

This hearty salad is great for lunch, or better yet, a midday picnic.

For convenience, the salad can be assembled a day or so in advance,

and ingredients can be subtracted or added at will.

The rich smoked chicken and fusilli

provide the backbone, and the anchovy vinaigrette and arugula give this dish its character and personality.

Occasionally I add pine nuts if I want crunch, or mushrooms if I want more substance,

but, really, almost anything can be added.

SERVES 8

10 anchovies, cleaned

1 teaspoon minced garlic

1 shallot, minced

¼ cup freshly squeezed
lemon juice

¾ cup olive oil

Salt and pepper

2 cups teardrop tomatoes

1 red onion, cut into
¼-inch-thick slices

2 zucchini, sliced crosswise
into ¼-inch-thick discs

3 small chicken breasts,
skin removed

4 tablespoons canola oil

2 cups dry hickory chips plus 1 cup
hickory chips soaked overnight in
water and drained

8 ounces dried fusilli pasta, cooked

3 cups baby arugula

METHOD—To prepare the vinaigrette: Purée the anchovies, garlic, shallot, lemon juice, and olive oil until smooth, and season to taste with salt and pepper.

To prepare the tomatoes: Prepare a charcoal grill. Wrap the tomatoes in aluminum foil and place on the grill for 10 to 15 minutes, or until they begin to pop open. Season to taste with salt and pepper.

To prepare the onions: Rub the onion slices with the remaining 2 tablespoons canola oil and season to taste with salt and pepper. Place on a hot grill for 5 to 8 minutes, or until tender. Let cool to room temperature.

To prepare the zucchini: Place the zucchini slices directly on a lightly oiled grill rack and cook for 3 minutes, or until the zucchini is cooked. Season to taste with salt and pepper.

To prepare the chicken breasts: Season the chicken with salt and pepper and brush with 2 tablespoons of the canola oil. Place the dry hickory chips over the hot coals in the grill. When the dry chips catch fire, sprinkle the wet chips over the coals. Place the chicken breasts on the grill and cover tightly with the grill lid. Smoke over medium heat for 5 minutes, turn the breasts over, and smoke for 5 to 7 minutes more, or until the chicken is cooked. Remove the chicken from the grill and thinly slice.

grilled chicken

fusilli

baby arugala

To prepare the salad: In a large bowl, toss the fusilli with the vinaigrette, chicken, red onion, tomatoes, and zucchini, and season to taste with salt and pepper.

ASSEMBLY—Arrange some of the arugula leaves in the center of each plate and spoon some of the pasta salad over the arugula.

WINE NOTES—This light, summery dish requires an equally light wine. A refreshing, summer-style Muscadet or the delicate smoke flavors of a lean Sonoma Chardonnay will both be perfect matches with this salad.

PUMPKIN TORTELLINI WITH BROWN BUTTER—BALSAMIC VINAIGRETTE

Tortellini and ravioli are really quite simple to make, even simpler if you make them with ready-to-go wonton skins. Here, the buttery pumpkin filling in these tortellini is highlighted by a nutty, **utterly delicious brown butter vinaigrette.** For texture a little bit of wilted spinach or Swiss chard works beautifully and can provide an important cleansing element. Not only can other hard winter squashes be substituted for the pumpkin, but chopped or ground shrimp or chicken work well too. These tortellini make for a fabulous appetizer, or they can work as a wonderful side dish for a main course.

SERVES 4

1 small pumpkin

1 tablespoon canola oil

½ teaspoon ground cinnamon

¼ teaspoon ground nutmeg

2 teaspoons sugar

Salt and pepper

Semolina Pasta (see page 215)

1 egg, lightly beaten

½ cup butter

2 tablespoons minced shallots

3 tablespoons balsamic vinegar

3 cups fresh baby spinach leaves

2 tablespoons julienned sage

METHOD—To prepare the pumpkin filling: Cut the pumpkin in half and scoop out the seeds. Rub the pumpkin flesh with the canola oil and season with the cinnamon and nutmeg. Place the pumpkin halves on a sheet pan with the cut side facing down and add ¼ inch of water to the pan. Roast the pumpkin at 350 degrees for 45 minutes, or until the pumpkin meat is tender.

Remove the pumpkin from the oven, let cool, and scrape out the flesh. Purée the pumpkin flesh and sugar in a food processor until smooth and season to taste with salt and pepper.

To assemble the tortellini: Roll out the Semolina Pasta into ¹⁄₁₆-inch-thick sheets. Cut the pasta sheets into twenty 3-inch squares. Place 1 heaping teaspoon of the pumpkin filling in the center of each pasta square. Lightly brush 2 sides of the pasta with the egg and fold the pasta in half, creating a triangle. Join the two ends of the long side of the triangle to form the tortellini, dab the seam with a touch of the egg, and firmly press the ends together to seal. Cook the tortellini in boiling salted water for 3 to 4 minutes, or until al dente.

fold in ends

assembling tortellini

To prepare the vinaigrette: Cook the butter over medium heat until it turns dark brown and has a nutty flavor. Remove from the heat, add the shallots and balsamic vinegar, and season to taste with salt and pepper.

To prepare the spinach: Place the spinach in a hot sauté pan with one-third of the vinaigrette and quickly wilt the spinach. Season to taste with salt and pepper.

ASSEMBLY—Place some of the wilted spinach in the center of each plate. Arrange 5 tortellini over the spinach and spoon some of the vinaigrette over the tortellini and around the plates. Sprinkle the sage around the plates and top with freshly ground black pepper.

WINE NOTES—The rich sweetness of the balsamic and pumpkin can be balanced out perfectly with rich fruit of a chardonnay. Mount Eden Vineyards from Santa Cruz has rich, ripe fruit and toasty oak, along with enough acidity to balance the pumpkin and vinaigrette.

This entree appeals in the most basic, soul-satisfying way. The toothsome linguine,

exotic mussels, crunchy asparagus, sharp leeks, heady morels,

and chewy pancetta achieve the pinnacle of their glory while swimming in the sensuous garlic-and saffron-

infused mussel broth. This combination of lusty flavors and

provocative textures compels you to eat slowly—

you simply do not want it to end. Serve this in small portions as an appetizer,

or in larger portions as a one-bowl meal with pieces of crusty bread.

SERVES 4

2 pounds mussels, cleaned and debearded

10 cloves garlic

⅛ teaspoon saffron threads

2 tablespoons minced shallots

2 cups white wine

2 cups Chicken Stock (see page 201)

2 tablespoons chopped fresh chives

2 tablespoons chopped fresh parsley leaves

Salt and pepper

2 cups morel mushrooms

1 tablespoon butter

½ cup diced pancetta

1 cup julienned leeks

12 asparagus spears, cleaned, blanched, and cut into 1½-inch pieces on the bias

8 ounces dried linguini, cooked and hot

METHOD—To prepare the mussels: Discard any mussels that have opened and do not close when gently tapped on the work surface. Bring the garlic, saffron, shallots, white wine, stock, chives, and parsley to a simmer. Add the mussels, cover with the lid, and cook for 3 to 5 minutes, or until all of the mussels have opened. (If a mussel does not open after cooking, throw it away.) Remove the mussels from the pan and simmer the liquid for 10 minutes, or until reduced by one-third. Season the cooking liquid to taste with salt and pepper.

To prepare the morels: Place the morels in a hot sauté pan over medium-high heat with the butter, pancetta, and leeks. Cook for 3 minutes, add the asparagus, and cook for 5 minutes, or until the morels are tender. Season to taste with salt and pepper.

ASSEMBLY—Place some of the warm linguini in the center of each bowl and top with some of the morel and asparagus mixture. Arrange several cooked mussels in each bowl. Pour the cooking liquid from the mussels into the bowls and top with freshly ground black pepper.

WINE NOTES—The delicate mineral flavors of the mussels echo those found in lean-style Chablis. A premier cru such as Vaillons or La Forêts from Moreau or Dauvissat marries perfectly with the myriad of flavors in this dish.

BLUE CHEESE RAVIOLI WITH BASIL-INFUSED TOMATO WATER

This elegant and light dish is ideal for blue cheese lovers.
The tomato, basil, onion, and blue cheese in the filling come together perfectly, with each flavor claiming its moment
on stage and then subtly yielding to another. Best of all is the experience of biting into the ravioli and
savoring the pungent, almost molten filling.
This dish can easily be converted into something more substantial
by adding duck or chicken or, perhaps, slices of grilled portobello mushrooms to the bowl and letting them swim with the ravioli.
The basil-infused tomato water is light and refreshing, but truly loaded with flavor.
And, for convenience it can be made a day or two ahead.

SERVES 4

10 large tomatoes, chopped

Salt

1 cup whole fresh basil leaves
plus 2 tablespoons fine chiffonade

2 cups red pearl onions, peeled

2 tablespoons butter

Pepper

1 cup blue cheese

2 tablespoons minced shallots

2 tablespoons chopped fresh chives

Semolina Pasta (see page 215)

1 egg, lightly beaten

METHOD—To prepare the tomato water: Purée the tomatoes in a food processor and season with salt. Tie the puréed tomatoes in cheesecloth and place the pouch in a colander on top of a pan. Refrigerate for 8 hours, or until all of the juices have dripped from the puréed tomatoes.

Discard the tomato purée and place the tomato water in a saucepan. Bring the liquid to a simmer, add the whole basil leaves, and remove the pan from the heat. Let the mixture steep for 5 minutes, remove the basil leaves, and season to taste with salt and pepper.

To prepare the onions: Place the pearl onions and butter in a small ovenproof pan and roast at 375 degrees for 45 to 60 minutes, or until the onions are golden brown and caramelized. Season to taste with salt and pepper.

To prepare the blue cheese filling: Mix the blue cheese, shallots, and chives until combined, and season to taste with salt and pepper.

To assemble the ravioli: Roll out the Semolina Pasta into $\frac{1}{16}$-inch-thick sheets. Cut the sheets into twenty-four $1\frac{1}{2}$-inch squares. Place 1 tablespoon of the blue cheese filling in the center of 12 of the pasta squares. Lightly brush the edges of the pasta squares with the egg and cover with another pasta square. Firmly press the edges of the pasta squares together to seal. Cook the ravioli in boiling salted water for 3 minutes, or until al dente, then drain.

tomato water

blue cheese ravioli

basil chiffonade

ASSEMBLY—Place some of the pearl onions in the center of each bowl. Arrange 3 blue cheese ravioli over the pearl onions and ladle in some of the tomato water. Sprinkle with the basil chiffonade and top with freshly ground black pepper.

WINE NOTES—A richer style of Chardonnay is needed here for the pungent blue cheese. Full-bodied Chardonnays such as Talbott and Mer Soliel have an intense and rich fruit flavor that is the perfect balance to the ravioli.

Chapter
9

Poultry

ROASTED CORNISH GAME HEN WITH POTATO PAVÉ
AND GINGERED MUSTARD SAUTERNES SAUCE

This preparation allows for the enjoyment of both the plump,

moist breast meat and the satisfying, crispy skin of this versatile small bird.

The accompanying pavé can be prepared a day or two ahead and reheated just before serving.

The Gingered Mustard Sauternes Sauce has a

sweet-sour quality to its basic flavor,

but its finish is far more complex. This dish can be plated individually

or served family-style on a platter with equally fabulous results.

SERVES 4

2 Idaho potatoes, peeled and thinly sliced

2 sweet potatoes, peeled and thinly sliced

3 cups heavy cream

5 tablespoons melted butter

Salt and pepper

1 tablespoon canola oil

4 rock Cornish game hens, trussed

8 sprigs thyme

2 cups haricots verts, blanched and cut into 1-inch pieces on the diagonal

Gingered Mustard Sauternes Sauce (see page 204)

2 tablespoons chopped fresh chervil

4 teaspoons Herb Oil, optional (see page 207)

20 strands Preserved Ginger (see page 211)

METHOD—To prepare the pavé: Place the Idaho and sweet potato slices in a large bowl, pour in the heavy cream, and gently toss to evenly coat the slices. Line an 8 by 8-inch pan with aluminum foil and brush the foil with ½ tablespoon of the melted butter. Arrange a layer of the Idaho potato slices in the bottom of the pan, overlapping them slightly, and season with salt and pepper. Arrange a layer of the sweet potato slices on top of the Idaho potatoes, overlapping them slightly, and season with salt and pepper. Continue alternating layers of Idaho and sweet potatoes until all of the potato slices are used. Tightly cover the pan with a second sheet of aluminum foil brushed with ½ tablespoon butter. Place another 8 by 8-inch pan over the foil and weight it down with a brick or other heavy, ovenproof object. Bake at 350 degrees for 1½ hours, or until the potatoes are tender. Leaving the weight on the pan, refrigerate the pavé for at least 4 hours.

Remove the pavé from the refrigerator. Remove the weight, the top pan, and the foil, and invert the potato pavé onto a sheet pan. Remove the foil and cut the pavé into 2-inch squares. Place 4 of the pavé squares in a large, nonstick sauté pan with the canola oil and cook over medium-high heat for 3 to 4 minutes, or until golden brown. Carefully turn the pavé and cook for 3 to 4 minutes, or until the pave is warmed through. (If the pavé is still not warm in the middle, it can be heated in a 375-degree oven for 5 minutes.)

To roast the hens: Season the rock Cornish game hens with salt and pepper and brush the skin with the remaining 4 tablespoons melted butter. Place a whole thyme sprig in the center cavity of each hen. Remove the leaves from the remaining thyme sprigs and sprinkle the leaves on the outside of the hens. Place the hens on a rack in a large roasting pan and roast at 375 degrees for 45 minutes, or until the juices run clear.

Remove the hens from the oven and allow them to rest for 10 minutes before carving the breasts and legs. (Save the carcasses for making a flavorful stock.)

ASSEMBLY—Place a piece of the pavé in the center of each plate. Arrange some of the meat from the hens at 4 points around the pavé. Place some of the haricots verts around the plate and spoon the Gingered Mustard Sauternes Sauce over the meat and around the plate. Sprinkle with the chopped chervil and top with freshly ground black pepper. Drizzle the Herb Oil around the plates and sprinkle with the Preserved Ginger.

WINE NOTES—This dish calls for a rich, aromatic white wine to balance with the ginger. Alsace Rieslings such as Meyer-Fonne's "Wineck-Schlossberg," Trimbach, or Domaine Weinbach will mesh beautifully.

GRILLED CHICKEN SALAD WITH CRUMBLED
BLUE CHEESE—LEMON VINAIGRETTE

This fairly quick presentation offers some **fascinating flavors and textures** and an enticing hot-cold temperature contrast. **While the chicken breasts are slowly grilling,** the salad ingredients can be arranged on the plates. The chicken breasts can then be transferred directly from the grill onto the salads. Beef or lamb would serve nicely in place of the chicken. If a vegetarian preparation were desired, grilled portobello mushrooms can be used in place of the meat.

SERVES 4

⅓ cup freshly squeezed lemon juice

1 cup olive oil

1½ cups crumbled Maytag blue cheese

Salt and pepper

2 cups frisée

2 cups baby arugula

2 cups mesclun mix

¾ cup walnuts, toasted

12 leaves Belgian endive

1 pear, peeled and thinly sliced

2 chicken breasts, grilled and sliced

METHOD—To make the vinaigrette: Place the lemon juice in a small bowl and slowly whisk in the olive oil. Whisk in 1 cup of the blue cheese and season to taste with salt and pepper.

To prepare the salad greens: Toss together the frisée, arugula, and mesclun in a medium bowl. Add the walnuts and the remaining ½ cup blue cheese.

ASSEMBLY—Arrange 3 endive leaves on one side of each plate and a few of the pear slices on the opposite side. Place some of the lettuce and blue cheese mixture in the center of each plate and top with several slices of the chicken breast. Drizzle some of the vinaigrette over the chicken and around the plate and top with freshly ground black pepper.

WINE NOTES—Semillon has the structure and richness necessary to balance the pungent flavor of the blue cheese. Full-bodied styles such as Carmenet White Meritage or Signorello Semillon are the perfect match.

CHICKEN DUMPLINGS WITH A STIR-FRY OF SHIITAKE MUSHROOMS, WATER CHESTNUTS, AND MUNG BEAN SPROUTS IN A GINGER-SOY-HIJIKI SAUCE

The textures of a variety of wonderful vegetables are celebrated in this dish. The crispy wontons and **vegetables superbly contrast and accentuate** the moist chicken filling. The Ginger-Soy-Hijiki Sauce seamlessly joins the vegetables and dumplings. More mushrooms can be added if an earthier result is desired. Or, for a lighter dish, you can convert it into a soup by using chicken or vegetable stock in place of the sauce.

SERVES 4

2 chicken breasts, skinned

2 tablespoons garlic chili paste

2 tablespoons hoisin sauce

3 tablespoons minced fresh ginger

1 jalapeño, seeded and minced

1 tablespoon minced garlic

Salt and pepper

16 small wonton wrappers

1 egg, whisked with 2 tablespoons water

Canola oil, for deep-frying

2 tablespoons canola oil

1 cup julienned carrots

1 cup shiitake mushrooms, julienned

1 cup julienned red bell peppers

1 cup julienned yellow bell peppers

½ cup thinly sliced water chestnuts

1 cup julienned leeks

1 cup mung bean sprouts

½ cup chopped scallions

2 tablespoons freshly squeezed lime juice

Ginger-Soy-Hijiki Sauce (see page 206)

3 tablespoons fresh cilantro leaves

4 tablespoons daikon sprouts

METHOD—To prepare the dumpling filling: Finely chop the chicken and toss in a large bowl with the garlic chile paste, hoisin sauce, 1 tablespoon of the ginger, the jalapeño, and ½ tablespoon of the garlic. Season to taste with salt and pepper. Sauté the chicken mixture for 5 to 7 minutes, or until all of the chicken is cooked. Let cool and adjust the season if necessary.

To prepare the dumplings: Lay the wonton wrappers out on a work surface. Lightly brush two adjoining edges of the wrappers with the egg mixture. Place 1½ tablespoons of the filling in the center of each wrapper. Fold the wontons in half on the diagonal, creating triangles, and gently press the sides together to seal. Heat the canola oil to 350 degrees in a large fry pan or wok. Fry the dumplings for 1 minute on each side, or until golden brown and crispy. Blot the dumplings on paper towels and season with salt.

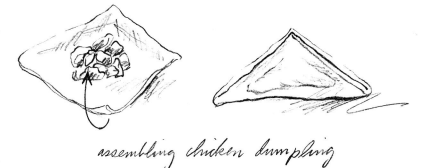

assembling chicken dumpling

131

To prepare the stir-fry: Sweat the remaining ½ tablespoon garlic and the remaining 2 tablespoons of ginger in the 2 tablespoons of canola oil in a wok over medium heat for 30 seconds. Add the carrots, mushrooms, and bell peppers and stir-fry for 1 minute. Add the water chestnuts, leeks, mung bean sprouts, and scallions and stir-fry for 2 minutes, or until all of the vegetables are just cooked. Remove from heat, add the lime juice, and season to taste with salt and pepper.

ASSEMBLY—Arrange some of the stir-fried vegetables in the center of each plate. Place 4 chicken dumplings on the vegetables. Spoon some of the Ginger-Soy-Hijiki Sauce over the dumplings and around the plate. Sprinkle the cilantro and daikon sprouts over the dumplings.

WINE NOTES—As an appetizer course, this spicy dish needs a full-bodied, toasty Champagne. Louis Roederer Brut premier is the perfect wine to cut the spice and begin a wonderful progression of wine. When serving this as an entrée, a full-bodied, oaky Chardonnay would be a perfect accompaniment.

GARLIC-BRAISED WHOLE CHICKEN WITH
FLAGEOLETS AND ROASTED LEEKS

This is truly a soul-satisfying combination of flavors and textures.
The tremendously tender chicken is sent over the top with the pungent garlic.
Melt-away flageolets dissolve in your mouth
like softened butter, offering only the slightest resistance, and the playful sharpness of the roasted leeks
offsets the other textures and flavors. This preparation works well as a casual family-style dish, or it can be
taken to the next level and served with black truffles or foie gras.

SERVES 4

One 3-to 4-pound chicken

Salt and pepper

4 bulbs garlic, cloves separated
and peeled

5 cups Chicken Stock (see page 201)

1½ cups flageolets, soaked overnight
in water

8 sage leaves

2 leeks, cut into 3-inch pieces

2 tablespoons butter

4 sprigs thyme

8 2-inch-diameter slices
sourdough bread

2 tablespoons olive oil

METHOD—To braise the chicken: Season the chicken with salt and pepper and slice the skin between the legs and breast so the legs lay flat. Place the garlic cloves, stock, flageolets, 4 of the sage leaves, and chicken in a pan. Roast at 325 degrees, stirring the liquid and basting the chicken every 20 minutes, for 2½ hours, or until the chicken is fork tender. Remove the chicken from the pan. Remove the leg and breast meat and thinly slice. Season the flageolets, garlic, and braising liquid to taste with salt and pepper.

To roast the leeks: Wrap the leeks, butter, and thyme sprigs tightly in a large piece of aluminum foil and roast at 325 degrees for 45 to 60 minutes, or until the leeks are tender. Remove from the oven and cut the leek pieces in half lengthwise. Season to taste with salt and pepper.

To prepare the croutons: Brush the bread with the oil, place on a sheet pan, and bake at 325 degrees for 15 minutes, or until lightly golden brown.

To prepare the sage: Julienne the 4 remaining sage leaves and reserve for garnish.

ASSEMBLY—Place 2 croutons in the center of each shallow bowl. Place some of the roasted leeks over the croutons and spoon the flageolets, garlic, and the cooking liquid over the leeks and in the bowl. Arrange some of the braised chicken over the leeks. Sprinkle the julienned sage leaves on the chicken and top with freshly ground black pepper.

WINE NOTES—The intensity of wines from Puligny-Montrachet helps neutralize the garlic's sharpness, yet leaves its delicate sweet flavor. Producers such as Etienne Sauzet and Domaine Leflaive will pair wonderfully with this dish.

133

MACADAMIA NUT—CRUSTED CHICKEN BREAST WITH LEMONGRASS—COCONUT EMULSION AND HERB OIL

This dish is rich and delicious,

with sensual flavors that harmonize perfectly.

The slightly wilted watercress

plays an important role in cutting the richness of the macadamia nuts and balancing all of the flavors.

If more substance is desired, noodles or rice can easily be added.

For an interesting variation, I sometimes substitute shellfish for the chicken,

but pork would work very well here, too.

SERVES 4

2 chicken breasts halved

Salt and pepper

¼ cup chopped macadamia nuts

2 tablespoons canola oil

2 cups watercress

2 cups coconut milk

1 cup milk

1 cup chopped lemongrass

1 tablespoon rice wine vinegar

1 tablespoon lemon juice

½ cup julienned Roasted Yellow Bell Pepper (see page 213)

½ cup julienned leek, blanched

¼ cup julienned fresh ginger, fried

2 tablespoons toasted coquitos shavings

8 teaspoons Herb Oil (see page 207)

METHOD—To prepare the chicken: Season the chicken breasts with salt and pepper and coat the top with the macadamia nuts to form a crust. Place the canola oil in a hot sauté pan, add the chicken, and cook for 3 minutes on each side, or until cooked through. Transfer the chicken to a plate.

To prepare the watercress: Add the watercress to the pan used for the chicken and gently cook for 1 minute. Season to taste with salt and pepper.

To prepare the emulsion: Simmer the coconut milk, milk, and lemongrass for 15 minutes. Strain the mixture through a sieve and discard the lemongrass. Return the liquid to the saucepan, add the vinegar and lemon juice, and mix with a handheld blender until frothy.

ASSEMBLY—Place some of the Roasted Yellow Bell Peppers and julienned leek in the center of each bowl. Arrange some of the wilted watercress over the vegetables and top with a chicken breast. Spoon some of the Lemongrass-coconut emulsion around the bowl and sprinkle with the fried ginger and toasted coquitos. Drizzle 2 teaspoons of the Herb Oil around the lemongrass-coconut emulsion in each bowl.

WINE NOTES—The tropical flavors in this dish call for an equally tropical flavored wine. ZD Chardonnay from California has delicate tropical overtones that beautifully echo the flavors in the emulsion.

TAMARIND–GLAZED ROASTED CHICKEN WITH APPLE–ONION–POTATO PURÉE

The tamarind glaze provides a refreshing,

sweet-sour tanginess

that perfectly highlights the succulent roasted chicken.

The apple-onion-potato purée acts as an elegant, satiny bed for the chicken pieces.

This is a great dish for the cool evenings of fall.

Braised celery or leeks would make a great accompanying vegetable

for this preparation.

SERVES 4

2 cups freshly squeezed orange juice

½ cup seedless tamarind paste

One 3-to 4-pound chicken, trussed

Salt and pepper

1 cup julienned Spanish onions

3½ tablespoons butter

1 Idaho potato, peeled, diced, and boiled

1 McIntosh apple, peeled, cored, and chopped

½ cup Chicken Stock (see page 201)

¼ cup heavy cream

1 McIntosh apple, thinly sliced

4 winter savory sprigs

4 baby thyme sprigs

METHOD—To make the tamarind glaze: Whisk the orange juice and tamarind paste over medium heat for 5 minutes, or until smooth.

To cook the chicken: Place the trussed chicken in a roasting pan and season with salt and pepper. Brush the chicken all over with the tamarind glaze and roast at 325 degrees for 60 to 90 minutes, or until the juices run clear. Brush on additional glaze every 15 minutes during the roasting. Cover the legs of the chicken with aluminum foil if they become too dark during roasting.

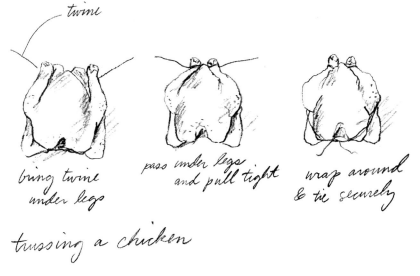

twine

bring twine under legs

pass under legs and pull tight

wrap around & tie securely

trussing a chicken

Bring the remaining tamarind glaze to a boil. Reduce to a simmer and cook for 5 minutes.

To make the purée: Cook the onions with ½ tablespoon of the butter over medium heat for 10 minutes, or until golden brown and caramelized. Remove two thirds of the onions and reserve them for garnish. Add the potato, chopped apple, and stock to the pan and simmer for 7 to 8 minutes, or until the apple is tender. Purée the mixture in a food processor with 2 tablespoons of butter and the cream until smooth. Season to taste with salt and pepper.

To prepare the apples: Sauté the apple slices in the remaining 1 tablespoon of butter over medium heat for 5 minutes, or until tender.

ASSEMBLY—Carve the chicken. Arrange some of the reserved caramelized onions, the apple slices, and roasted chicken in the center of each plate. Spoon a ring of the purée around the chicken and spoon the tamarind glaze over the chicken and around the plate. Garnish with the reserved onion, savory, and thyme sprigs and top with freshly ground black pepper.

WINE NOTES—The rich fruit of an American Pinot Blanc is the perfect balance for the apple and caramelized onion in the potato purée. Etude from Carneros has rich fruit and a fair amount of oak that will wonderfully complement the tamarind on the chicken.

Chapter

10

Pork

DRIED FRUIT—STUFFED PORK TENDERLOIN
WITH ROASTED NEW POTATOES AND
BACON—SHERRY VINAIGRETTE

Intensely flavored dried fruit really seems to bring out the clean, delicate qualities of pork.

Furthermore, the dried fruits provide a

sweetness, tartness, and acidity

that showcase the meat and provide a balance to the bacon-flavored potatoes

and the luscious, slightly bitter endive. The flavors in this dish perform in unison

and exquisite harmony. This preparation works as well as part of a formal dinner as it does

as a simple everyday meal for the family.

SERVES 4

2 pounds new red potatoes, halved

½ cup plus 3 tablespoons olive oil

6 sprigs fresh thyme leaves

Salt and pepper

⅓ cup dried cranberries

⅓ cup dried golden raisins

⅓ cup chopped dried apricots

⅓ cup dried currants

4 tablespoons julienned
fresh sage leaves

½ cup water

1 20-ounce pork tenderloin,
cleaned and halved

3 tablespoons canola oil

1 large head radicchio, quartered

1 tablespoon butter

2 teaspoons sugar

½ cup Chicken Stock (see page 201)

½ cup uncooked bacon batons

½ cup minced red onion

1 teaspoon minced garlic

2½ tablespoons sherry wine vinegar

METHOD—To prepare the potatoes: Toss the potatoes with 3 tablespoons of the olive oil and the thyme leaves and season with salt and pepper. Place on a roasting pan or sheet pan and roast at 375 degrees for 45 to 60 minutes, or until the potatoes are golden brown and crispy, turning them once to ensure even browning.

To prepare the filling: Cook the cranberries, raisins, apricots, currants, 2 tablespoons of the sage, and the water in a medium saucepan over low heat for 5 minutes, or until warm. Remove from the heat and let stand for 15 minutes.

To prepare the pork tenderloin: Starting from the end of each half of tenderloin, cut a slit along the center using a sharp boning knife or other thin knife. If the knife is not long enough to reach the far end of the loins, repeat the process starting from the other end. Turn the loins on their sides and cut another slit to create an "X" in the center of the loins. Insert the handle of a long wooden spoon through the incision to help stretch the hole. Using your fingers and the wooden spoon handle, stuff as much filling as possible into each loin. Season the outside of the loins with salt and pepper.

Place the canola oil in a hot sauté pan over high heat. Add the pork loin and sear on all sides. Reduce the heat to medium-high and cook for 5 minutes on each side, or until the pork registers 150 degrees on a meat thermometer. Let rest for 10 minutes before slicing.

stuffing a tenderloin

insert thin knife
cut slit

rotate and
create x

insert spoon
to enlarge hole

To prepare the radicchio: Cook the radicchio and butter in a large sauté pan over medium heat for 3 to 4 minutes, or until it starts to caramelize. Add the sugar and stock, cover, and cook for 5 to 10 minutes, or until the radicchio is tender. Season to taste with salt and pepper.

To prepare the bacon-sherry vinaigrette: Render the bacon in a sauté pan over medium heat. Add the red onion and garlic and cook for 1 minute, or until the red onion is softened. Remove from heat and add the sherry wine vinegar and the remaining 2 tablespoons of sage. Slowly whisk in the remaining ½ cup of olive oil and season to taste with salt and pepper.

ASSEMBLY—Place some of the radicchio in the center of each plate and arrange some of the roasted potatoes around the radicchio. Cut the stuffed pork tenderloin into ¼-inch-thick slices and place 3 slices on top of the radicchio on each plate. Spoon the bacon-sherry vinaigrette over the pork and around the plate and top with freshly ground black pepper.

WINE NOTES—The dried fruits add acidity to this dish, and the pork and vinaigrette scream out for ripe, spicy flavors in a wine. Zinfandels from producers such as Ravenswood and Ridge are intense styles that will fit the mold for this dish.

THAI BARBECUE—BRAISED BOAR CHOPS WITH JASMINE RICE AND SHIITAKE MUSHROOMS

If you can get a hold of boar chops, try this gutsy and extraordinarily satisfying preparation. The sweet, sour, and hot barbecue sauce thoroughly saturates the meat during the braising process, making each bite a luscious, zingy explosion of exotic flavor. The boar meat stands up to these assertive flavors and is perfectly supported by the delicate backdrop of the jasmine rice. Shiitake mushrooms provide a diversion of texture and flavor, keeping the entire plate in balance. Lamb chops or ordinary pork chops also work well, although both benefit from more conservative saucing.

SERVES 4

8 boar chops

Salt and pepper

2 tablespoons canola oil

½ cup chopped red bell peppers

½ cup chopped green bell peppers

½ cup chopped yellow bell peppers

1 tablespoon Szechwan peppercorns

½ cup chopped onion

Thai Barbecue Sauce (see page 218)

1 quart Chicken Stock (see page 201)

3 cups shiitake mushrooms, stemmed and quartered

1 tablespoon minced shallots

1 tablespoon butter

4 cups cooked jasmine rice, hot

¼ cup fresh cilantro leaves

METHOD—To prepare the boar chops: Season the chops with salt and pepper and sear in a large roasting pan in the canola oil over medium-high heat for 1 to 2 minutes on each side, or until caramelized. Remove the chops and add the red, green, and yellow bell peppers, the peppercorns, and onion to the pan. Cook over high heat for 2 to 3 minutes, or until caramelized. Return the chops to the pan and cover with the Thai Barbecue Sauce and the stock. Bring the mixture to a simmer and cover with a lid. Reduce to very low heat and cook for 2½ to 3 hours, or until the chops are extremely tender and the meat is almost falling off the bone. Carefully remove the boar chops from the braising liquid, strain the liquid, and discard the solids. Place the braising liquid in a saucepan and simmer for 15 to 20 minutes, or until reduced to about 2 cups.

To prepare the mushrooms: Cook the shiitake mushrooms, shallots, and butter over medium-high heat for 3 to 5 minutes, or until the mushrooms are tender. Season to taste with salt and pepper.

ASSEMBLY—Place a large spoonful of the jasmine rice in the center of each plate and place 2 boar chops over the rice. Arrange some of the shiitake mushrooms around the plate. Spoon some of the braising liquid over the chops and around the plate and sprinkle with the cilantro leaves.

WINE NOTES—The barbecue sauce in this dish adds a sweetness that can be balanced by the ripe tannins of the Syrah grape. American Syrah has rich fruit, ripe tannins, and finishes with a delicate spice that is fabulous with the boar. Ojai's Bien Nacido Vineyard Syrah is a perfect match.

ROASTED PORK TENDERLOIN WITH
JUNIPER-INFUSED RED CABBAGE

This is one of the most simple and straightforward preparations I can imagine.
The pork loin is roasted on a bed of apple and onion,
which not only perfumes the meat with marvelous flavor but acts as a perfect accompaniment.
The juniper-flavored cabbage is delicious
in its own right, but it also provides a backdrop that superbly spotlights and cuts into the flavor of the meat.
Sweet potatoes round out this dish and provide a natural, mild sweetness
that amplifies the elegance of the pork.
Sometimes, for variety, I'll add chiles or ginger to the cabbage.

SERVES 4

1 1½-pound pork tenderloin

Salt and pepper

4 tablespoons chopped
fresh parsley leaves

2 tablespoons chopped
fresh thyme leaves

2 Granny Smith apples, chopped

2 Spanish onions, chopped

3 sweet potatoes, peeled and cut into
½-inch-thick slices

¼ cup butter

¾ cup maple syrup

½ cup uncooked diced bacon

4 cups chopped red cabbage

1 teaspoon ground juniper berries

3 tablespoons red wine

4 tablespoons balsamic vinegar

1 cup water

METHOD—To prepare the pork: Season the tenderloin with salt and pepper and pat on 2 tablespoons of the parsley and the thyme. Place the apples and onions in a roasting pan and lay the pork loin on top. Roast in the oven at 450 degrees for 10 minutes, lower the temperature to 350 degrees, and cook for 30 minutes, or until the pork has an internal temperature of 150 degrees. Allow the pork to rest for 10 minutes before slicing.

To cook the sweet potatoes: Place the sweet potatoes in an ovenproof baking pan. Add 2 tablespoons of the butter and the maple syrup to the pan and cover with aluminum foil or a tight-fitting lid. Bake at 375 degrees for 20 minutes. Remove the lid from the pan, baste the potatoes with the cooking liquid, and cook uncovered for 20 minutes, or until the potatoes are tender. Remove from the oven and season the sweet potatoes with salt and pepper.

To prepare the cabbage: Render the bacon in a large sauté pan. Add the cabbage and ground juniper berries and cook for 3 minutes. Add the red wine and balsamic vinegar and cook until the wine and vinegar are almost cooked out. Add the water and cook for 10 minutes, or until the cabbage is tender. Remove the cabbage from the pan, reserving the cooking liquid. Season to taste with salt and pepper.

To prepare the sauce: Pour the juices from the sweet potatoes into the cooking liquid from the cabbage. Add the remaining 2 tablespoons parsley and whisk in the remaining 2 tablespoons butter. Season to taste with salt and pepper.

ASSEMBLY—Place some of the braised red cabbage in the center of each plate. Arrange some of the sweet potato slices over the cabbage. Slice the pork loin and arrange a few slices over the sweet potatoes. Spoon the sauce over the pork slices and around the plates.

WINE NOTES—The cabbage adds an acidity to this dish that is a refreshing complement to the sweet potato. A well-rounded Chardonnay such as Au Bon Climat's "Talley Vineyard" from Arroyo Grande keeps the vegetables in balance and beautifully complements the meat.

roasted pork loin

cabbage

sauce

GRILLED PORK CHOPS WITH PICKLED RED ONIONS AND FIG–BALSAMIC SAUCE

These robust chops get their kick from thickly cut slices of pickled red onions, which also add a tremendous textural quality. A mixture of corn and black beans adds substance and a rich, deep flavor, which is balanced by the slightly sweet fig and balsamic sauce which is also spiked with black pepper and vanilla. The sauce, corn, beans, and pickled onions can all be prepared ahead of time, so the entire dish literally comes together as quickly as the pork chops can be grilled.

SERVES 4

8 ounces dried figs

3 tablespoons balsamic vinegar

¾ cup olive oil

1 cup water

Pulp of ½ vanilla bean

1 teaspoon freshly ground black pepper, plus additional

Salt

4 large center-cut pork chops

½ cup diced Spanish onions

2 cups sweet corn kernels

2 tablespoons butter

2 cups cooked black beans

½ cup small-diced red bell peppers

2 tablespoons chopped fresh parsley leaves

Pickled Red Onion Rings (recipe follows)

METHOD—To prepare the fig sauce: Purée the figs, balsamic vinegar, olive oil, water, vanilla bean pulp, and 1 tablespoon freshly ground black pepper until smooth. Strain through a fine-mesh sieve and season to taste with salt and pepper.

To prepare the pork chops: Season the pork chops with salt and pepper and brush with some of the fig sauce. Grill for 4 minutes on each side, or until cooked.

To prepare the corn: Sauté the onions and corn in the butter over medium heat for 5 minutes. Add the black beans, red bell peppers, and parsley and cook for 5 minutes. Season to taste with salt and pepper.

ASSEMBLY—Warm the remaining fig sauce over medium heat for 5 minutes, or until heated through. Arrange some of the Pickled Red Onion Rings in the center of each plate and top with some of the corn–black bean mixture. Place a pork chop over the mixture and spoon the remaining fig sauce around the plate and top with freshly ground black pepper.

WINE NOTES—The figs and pepper in this dish add flavors that lean toward Rhone varietals. Syrah, from the northern Rhone, has roasted fruit flavors and a wonderful aroma of cracked pepper that echoes those in the dish. Try a Saint-Joseph from Alain Gaillot or Jean Louis Chave.

grilled pork chop

corn-black bean mixture

fig-balsamic sauce

Pickled Red Onion Rings

The onions can be stored in the pickling juice for up to 1 week.

YIELD: ABOUT 1 CUP

1 red onion, cut into
⅛-inch-thick rings

½ cup water

½ cup rice wine vinegar

¼ cup sugar

1 tablespoon kosher salt

1 clove

1 teaspoon mustard seeds

1 teaspoon black peppercorns

1 teaspoon peeled,
chopped fresh ginger

METHOD—Combine all of the ingredients in a small saucepan and simmer for 5 minutes, or until the salt and sugar dissolve. Remove from the heat and steep for 20 minutes. Remove the red onion rings from the liquid. (The pickling juice may be stored in the refrigerator and reserved for another use.)

CHILLED PORK SALAD WITH WALNUTS, CANTALOUPE, JICAMA, AND CUMIN VINAIGRETTE

This preparation makes a great mid-day meal. The cantaloupe, watercress, and jicama work together nicely to contrast the mild flavor and firmness of the chilled meat. Roasted cumin seeds in the vinaigrette add an exotic flavor that pushes this combination over the top. Peaches, plums, figs, and apples could work nicely in place of the cantaloupe, and if you prefer something with less bite, try mâche or Boston lettuce instead of watercress. Also, it's a great way to use leftover pork. Lamb or beef work well here too.

SERVES 4

4 teaspoons cumin seeds, toasted and coarsely ground

4½ tablespoons raspberry vinegar

¼ cup olive oil

⅓ cup walnut oil

Salt and pepper

2 thick-cut boneless pork chops (or pork loin)

2 tablespoons canola oil

1 red onion, julienned

1 tablespoon butter

4 cups watercress, stemmed

2 cups julienned cantaloupe

½ cup walnuts, toasted and chopped

1 cup peeled and julienned jicama

METHOD—To prepare the vinaigrette: Place the cumin and raspberry vinegar in a small bowl and slowly whisk in the olive oil and walnut oil. Season to taste with salt and pepper.

To prepare the pork: Season the pork with salt and pepper. Place the canola oil in a hot sauté pan over high heat and sear the pork for 2 to 3 minutes on each side, or until golden brown. Reduce the heat to medium, cover, and cook for 5 to 7 minutes, or until the pork has an internal temperature of 150 degrees. Reserve any pan juices and refrigerate the meat for 1 hour, or until completely chilled. Thinly slice the pork and season to taste with salt and pepper.

To prepare the onions: Cook the onion in the butter over medium-high heat for 5 minutes or until golden and caramelized. Season to taste with salt and pepper.

To prepare the salad: Toss together the watercress, onions, cantaloupe, walnuts, jicama, and three-quarters of the vinaigrette. Season to taste with salt and pepper.

ASSEMBLY—Place some of the salad in the center of each plate and top with a few of the pork slices. Spoon the remaining vinaigrette and pan juices over the pork and around the plates. Top with freshly ground black pepper.

WINE NOTES—Wines with melon flavors and full acidity will marry well with the dish. Rieslings from Western Australia such as Leeuwin Estate and Franklin Estate have delicate melon flavors and bright acidity that complement the cumin and stand up to the pork.

151

SHREDDED PORK WITH WILD RICE PANCAKES
AND PECAN SAUCE

This shredded pork preparation is similar to rillettes, but without all the fat to mask the flavor of the meat. Delicate pancakes provide a splendid accompaniment to the pork, with the nuttiness and texture of the wild rice perfectly complementing the shredded meat. A playfully spicy pecan sauce adds depth of flavor that gives the entire dish substance. This satisfying dish can work either as an appetizer or as an entrée. Roasted potatoes work well as an accompaniment instead of the wild rice pancakes.

SERVES 4

¾ pound boneless pork loin

Salt and pepper

1 cup chopped Spanish onions

1 cup chopped leeks

½ cup chopped carrots

½ cup chopped celery

½ cup chopped red bell peppers

2 jalapeños, seeded and chopped

3 tablespoons peeled, chopped
fresh ginger

3 cloves garlic

2 tablespoons canola oil

3 cups Chicken Stock (see page 201)

½ cup chopped dried cherries

4 tablespoons chopped
fresh marjoram

½ cup pecans, toasted and chopped

2 tablespoons vinegar

3 tablespoons butter

Wild Rice Pancakes (recipe follows)

METHOD—To prepare the pork: Season the pork with salt and pepper. Sauté the onions, leeks, carrots, celery, bell peppers, jalapeños, ginger, and garlic with the canola oil in a small roasting pan over medium heat for 10 minutes, or until the vegetables are caramelized. Place the pork on top of the vegetables and roast at 450 degrees for 10 minutes. Reduce the temperature to 300 degrees. Add the stock and enough water to cover three-quarters of the pork and cover the pan with aluminum foil. Roast the pork, basting every 30 minutes, for 2½ to 3 hours, or until tender when pierced with a fork.

Remove the pork from the braising liquid and set aside to cool slightly. Strain the braising liquid through a fine-mesh sieve. Shred the pork into small pieces with a fork, add the dried cherries and 2 tablespoons of marjoram, and season to taste with salt and pepper.

To prepare the sauce: Simmer the braising liquid for 20 minutes, or until reduced to 1¼ cups. Remove ½ cup of braising liquid and add it to the pork. Add the pecans, the remaining 2 tablespoons marjoram, and vinegar to the remaining liquid and whisk in the butter. Season with salt and pepper.

ASSEMBLY—Place 3 of the Wild Rice Pancakes in the center of each plate and arrange some of the shredded pork on top of the pancakes. Spoon some of the sauce over the pork and around the plate.

wild rice pancakes

shredded pork

pecan sauce

WINE NOTES—The nut flavors of the pork need a wine with nutty flavors. Hermitage Blanc takes on a delicate nutty flavor that meshes well with the pecan sauce and pork. Try one from a producer such as Sorrel or Jean Louis Chave.

Wild Rice Pancakes

These pancakes are also great for breakfast.

YIELD: ABOUT 15 PANCAKES

1 tablespoon chopped onions

2 teaspoons walnut oil

1 teaspoon butter

1 egg

1 egg yolk

½ cup milk

½ cup flour

1 tablespoon baking powder

Pinch of salt

¾ cup cooked wild rice

¼ cup chopped scallions

½ cup chopped dried cherries

1 tablespoon chopped parsley

Canola oil, for cooking

METHOD—Sauté the onions in the walnut oil and butter for 2 to 3 minutes, or until light golden brown. Place the egg, egg yolk, and milk in a medium bowl and whisk together until well blended. Sift together the flour, baking powder, and salt, add the egg mixture, and whisk until smooth. Fold in the wild rice, cooked onions, scallions, dried cherries, and parsley. Spoon 2 tablespoons of the pancake batter into a lightly oiled nonstick sauté pan and cook the pancake for 1 minute on each side. Repeat this process with the remaining pancake batter.

Chapter 11

Duck

CRISPY DUCK CONFIT WITH POTATO PURÉE, COLLARD GREENS, AND DUCK JUS

One of the most satisfying, comforting, even sensual gastronomic pleasures is savoring melt-away duck confit, and it's actually fairly simple to make. Once the meat has cured for a couple of days, it only needs to be slowly "poached" in fat. Here it is served with tangy, earthy collard greens, some satiny potatoes, and a little drizzle of duck stock. This dish is pure bliss.

SERVES 4

½ cup chopped uncooked bacon

4 cups chopped collard greens

1 tablespoon sugar

2 tablespoons red wine vinegar

½ cup water

Salt and pepper

1½ pounds Yukon Gold potatoes, peeled and chopped

1 cup milk, hot

½ cup butter

Duck Confit (see page 203)

Duck Jus (see page 204)

4 teaspoons tiny basil leaves

1 teaspoon fleur de sel (French sea salt)

METHOD—To prepare the greens: Render the bacon in a medium sauté pan and add the collard greens. Cook for 3 minutes, add the sugar, red wine vinegar, and water, and continue to cook for 10 minutes or until the greens are tender. Season to taste with salt and pepper.

To prepare the potatoes: Cook the potatoes in boiling salted water until tender. Drain and pass through a ricer. Place in a mixing bowl, with the milk and butter, and whip until smooth. Season to taste with salt and pepper.

ASSEMBLY—Place some of the collard greens in the center of each plate. Place a piece of the crispy Duck Confit on top of the collard greens and spoon a ring of potato purée around the plate. Spoon some of the jus over the confit, sprinkle with the basil, fleur de sel, and pepper.

WINE NOTES—The melt-in-your-mouth texture of the duck in this dish is accentuated by the earthiness and full acidity of a Grenache grape. Richness is also needed to offset the delicately bitter flavor of the collard greens. Wines from the producer Raspail-Ay from Gigondas are fine examples of this varietal and will match perfectly with this dish.

DUCK BREAST SALAD WITH WILTED GREENS, WARM GOAT CHEESE, AND WALNUT VINAIGRETTE

A dish like this can be prepared in a
rustic or elegant manner with the same fabulous results. The goat cheese is so creamy
it simply melts in your mouth—
the perfect foil to the crunchy walnuts.
The Apple-Mango Chutney adds its complex flavors and a luscious mouth-feel, and the pan
vinaigrette brings in just the right note of acid.
This is a great preparation for duck, but it also works well with beef.

SERVES 4

4 medium duck breasts, skin on

Salt and pepper

4 1½-ounce medallions goat cheese

1 egg, lightly whisked with
2 tablespoons water

1 cup bread crumbs

2 tablespoons canola oil

¼ cup red wine vinegar

⅓ cup walnuts, toasted and chopped

4 cups mesclun greens, cleaned

Apple-Mango Chutney
(recipe follows)

¼ cup snow pea sprouts

4 teaspoons thyme leaves

METHOD—To prepare the duck: Carefully score the fatty skin of the duck in a grid fashion, being careful not to pierce the flesh. Season with salt and pepper. Place in a hot sauté pan, skin side down first, and cook for 4 minutes on each side, or until the skin is golden brown and crispy and the duck is cooked medium. Remove the breasts from the pan and strain and reserve the fat. Allow the duck breasts to rest for 5 minutes before slicing into 4 pieces.

To prepare the goat cheese medallions: Dip the goat cheese in the egg mixture and completely cover with the bread crumbs, making sure they are firmly attached. Place the canola oil in a preheated sauté pan and add the goat cheese medallions. Cook for 2 minutes on each side, or until golden brown.

To prepare the vinaigrette: Reserve 2 tablespoons of the duck fat and place the remaining fat in a small bowl. Whisk in the red wine vinegar. Using the back side of a chef's knife, smash ¼ cup of the toasted walnuts into a purée. Add the nuts to the vinaigrette and season to taste with salt and pepper.

To prepare the greens: Place the mesclun greens and the reserved duck fat in a medium pan and quickly wilt the greens over medium heat. Season to taste with salt and pepper and fold in the remaining 1⅓ tablespoons walnuts.

ASSEMBLY—Arrange some of the wilted greens in the center of each plate and place 4 slices of duck breast around the plate. Top with a crispy goat cheese medallion. Spoon the duck fat vinaigrette and some of the Apple-Mango Chutney around the plates and sprinkle with the snow pea sprouts. Top with freshly ground black pepper.

WINE NOTES—The delicate, nutty flavor of an Hermitage Blanc by Jean Louis Chave is a fabulous accompaniment to the goat cheese. The rich texture from the Roussanne grape that it's made from holds up well to the richness of the duck.

Apple-Mango Chutney

You can make a large batch of this and can it for other uses.

YIELD: ABOUT 1 CUP

1/4 cup onion, chopped

1 tablespoon peeled, chopped fresh ginger

1 tablespoon canola oil

1/2 cup diced ripe mango

1/2 cup diced unripe mango

1/2 cup Granny Smith apple, peeled, cored, and chopped

2 tablespoons dried cranberries

2 tablespoons dried black currants

1 cinnamon stick

1 star anise

2 tablespoons small-diced red bell pepper

2 tablespoons seeded small-diced jalapeño pepper

2 tablespoons small-diced green bell pepper

1/4 cup rice wine vinegar

1/4 cup sugar

1/4 cup water

METHOD—Sauté the chopped onion and ginger in the canola oil in a medium saucepan over medium heat for 2 to 3 minutes, or until translucent. Add the remaining ingredients and stir until combined. Cook over medium-low heat, stirring occassionally, for 1 1/2 hours, or until all of the liquid has been cooked out of the chutney. Remove the star anise and cinnamon stick. This can be made ahead of time and reheated just prior to use.

STIR-FRY OF SESAME OIL—MARINATED DUCK AND SHIITAKE MUSHROOMS WITH STAR ANISE— PLUM SAUCE

The great thing about a stir-fry is that once you
have everything cut up, it takes just moments to put the dish together.
In this particular preparation you will enjoy the marvelous textures
and flavors of all the vegetables, but you will truly revel in the
hauntingly elegant taste of the star anise–plum sauce.
This dish works nicely as an appetizer, or you can add rice or cellophane noodles
to make it a more substantial dish.
For a variation, try substituting lobster or shrimp for the duck.

SERVES 4

3 duck breasts, skin removed

½ cup sesame oil

4 star anise, broken into pieces

3 ripe plums, peeled and chopped

2 tablespoons sugar

½ cup water

2 tablespoons Spicy Vinegar
(see page 217)

Salt and pepper

2 tablespoons peeled, chopped
fresh ginger

2 tablespoons chopped garlic

1 bunch scallions, cleaned and cut
into 1½-inch pieces on the diagonal

2 cups julienned shiitake mushrooms

½ cup water chestnuts, diced

1 red bell pepper, julienned

1 yellow bell pepper, julienned

2 cups bok choy, coarsely chopped

2 teaspoons sesame seeds

2 tablespoons chopped cilantro

METHOD—To prepare the duck: Cut the duck breasts into small strips and toss with the sesame oil and half the star anise. Let sit in the refrigerator for at least 2 hours and then remove the star anise pieces.

To prepare the sauce: Place the plums, remaining star anise, sugar, and water in a small saucepan and cook over medium heat for 4 to 5 minutes, or until the plums are tender. Place the mixture in the blender and purée for 3 minutes, or until smooth. Pass through a fine-mesh sieve, stir in the Spicy Vinegar, and season to taste with salt and pepper. Keep warm.

In a preheated wok or large sauté pan, cook the duck, ginger, and garlic for 2 to 3 minutes. Add the scallions and cook for 2 minutes, then add the mushrooms, water chestnuts, and bell peppers, and continue to stir-fry for 2 to 3 minutes, or until the duck is cooked and the vegetables are tender. Add the bok choy and season to taste with salt and pepper. Remove from heat and stir in the sesame seeds.

ASSEMBLY—Place some of the stir-fried duck mixture in the center of each plate and spoon the star anise–plum sauce around the stir-fry. Sprinkle with the chopped cilantro and spoon any of the cooking juices from the wok over the stir-fry to moisten the duck.

WINE NOTES—The aromatic star anise and sweet flavors from the plum sauce are balanced wonderfully by an Alsace Gewurztraminer. They have a little bit of sweetness that cuts throught the light spice of the dish. Domaine Weinbach and Etienne Hugel make crisp examples of this varietal.

161

SAUTÉED DUCK BREAST WITH WILTED SPINACH
AND GINGER-BRAISED RHUBARB

The clear, refreshing flavor of rhubarb

perfectly accents the plump, luscious meat of the duck breasts.

Ginger provides an additional zip and further accentuates the meat.

Wilted spinach, or almost any type of braised greens, add a playful foil,

and all that's really needed to round out this preparation

is a little meat juice. Other birds, especially richer ones such as squab or pheasant,

may easily be substituted for the duck. Seared foie gras would also make

a tremendous substitution.

SERVES 4

2 tablespoons butter

1 1-inch piece ginger, peeled

4 large stalks rhubarb, cut into
1-inch pieces on the diagonal

2 teaspoons sugar

1 cup Chicken Stock
(see page 201)

2 tablespoons Preserved Ginger
(see page 211)

Salt and pepper

4 duck breasts, trimmed
and skin scored

3 cups chopped spinach or
Swiss chard, cleaned

METHOD—To prepare the rhubarb: Place the butter, ginger, rhubarb, sugar, and ¾ cup of the stock in a medium pan and cook over medium-low heat for 5 to 6 minutes, or until the rhubarb is tender. Remove from the heat, remove the ginger, add the Preserved Ginger, and season to taste with salt and pepper. Purée one-third of the rhubarb and all of the cooking liquid for 1 to 2 minutes, or until smooth.

Season the duck breasts with salt and pepper and place in a very hot sauté pan with the skin side down first. Cook for 4 minutes on each side, or until the skin is golden brown and crispy and the duck is cooked medium. Remove from the pan and allow the duck to rest for 5 minutes, and thinly slice. Drain the fat from the pan reserving any juices. Place the Swiss chard in the pan from the duck and quickly wilt with the remaining ¼ cup of stock. Season to taste with salt and pepper.

ASSEMBLY—Place some of the Swiss chard in the center of each plate and top with some of the rhubarb pieces. Arrange the duck breast slices on top of the rhubarb and spoon the rhubarb sauce and duck juices around the plates. Top with freshly ground black pepper.

WINE NOTES—The tart sweetness of the rhubarb in this dish will be complemented by a wine with rich fruit. Zinfandel pairs marvelously with the rhubarb and has a wonderful spice that accentuates the duck. Ravenswood from Sonoma makes many different styles of Zinfandel and is easily accessible.

PEPPERCORN–CRUSTED WHOLE ROASTED DUCK

Whole roasting is the simplest process for cooking duck,

and it helps the meat retain more of its natural flavor and succulence.

In this version, a pungent, peppery crust nicely balances the rich meat,

while the sweet-hot sauce acts as the perfect foil to the rich skin.

Roasted sweet potatoes or perhaps some braised legumes

are all that is needed to finish this preparation.

SERVES 4

1 tablespoon cracked
black peppercorns

1 tablespoon cracked
green peppercorns

1 tablespoon cracked
white peppercorns

½ cup olive oil

1 tablespoon chopped garlic

Salt and pepper

1 medium whole duck, cleaned

1 large onion, quartered

2 carrots, peeled and chopped

2 stalks celery, chopped

½ cup Chicken Stock
(see page 201)

2 tablespoons chopped chives

¼ cup Black Olive–Caper Vinaigrette
(see page 200)

4 tablespoons whole-grain mustard

¼ cup butter

METHOD—To prepare the duck: Combine the cracked peppercorns, olive oil, and garlic and season with salt. Season the inner cavity of the duck with salt and pepper and trim any excess fat. Pierce the skin of the duck with a fork 10 to 15 times to release the fat during cooking. Brush the cracked peppercorn mixture all over the outside of the duck, reserving any extra to use while roasting. Place the onion, carrots, and celery in a roasting pan and place the duck on top of the vegetables. Roast at 400 degrees for 15 minutes, reduce the temperature to 350 degrees, and continue to cook for about 45 to 60 minutes, basting occasionally with the remaining peppercorn mixture and any drippings, until golden brown and crispy and the juice from the cavity runs clear. Remove the duck from the oven and allow to rest for 15 minutes before carving.

To prepare the sauce: Drain the juices from the pan into a clear glass and drain off all of the fat. There will only be about ¼ cup of juices remaining. Place the juices in a small saucepan with the stock, chives, and the Black Olive–Caper Vinaigrette. Cook over medium heat for 2 to 3 minutes, or until warm. Remove from the heat, whisk in the butter, and season to taste with salt and pepper.

ASSEMBLY—Slice the duck and place some in the center of each plate. Spoon some of the sauce over and around the duck.

WINE NOTES—The pungence of the pepper in this dish can be balanced by the "raisiny" flavors in some wines. Amarone from a producer such as Masi has rich, raisiny fruit and a higher alcohol that also matches well with the duck.

GRILLED DUCK BREAST WITH BRAISED ENDIVE, ROASTED APPLES, AND RED WINE JUS

Duck is especially delicious when grilled

over a fire. Alder, cherry, hickory, or mesquite all add a depth to the meat.

Here the flavor is tamed with the bitter endive and the sweet apple.

The Red Wine Jus keeps all the flavors in line

and even elevates them in its complex fruitiness.

This preparation can be made with almost any type of poultry,

or even with pork.

SERVES 4

4 small duck breasts, cleaned and skin scored

Salt and pepper

1 tablespoon canola oil

3 Granny Smith apples, peeled, cored, and cut into ½-inch rings

4 tablespoons butter

6 sage leaves

3 tablespoons firmly packed brown sugar

2 heads Belgian endive, quartered

1 tablespoon sugar

1½ cups Chicken Stock (see page 201)

Red Wine Jus (see page 213)

METHOD—To prepare the duck: Season the duck breasts with salt and pepper. Lightly brush them with oil and place on a grill over a medium flame. Cook for 3 to 4 minutes on each side, or until cooked to the desired doneness. Let rest for 3 minutes before slicing.

To prepare the apples: Place the apple rings in an ovenproof pan with 2 tablespoons butter, 3 sage leaves, and the brown sugar. Cover and bake at 350 degrees for 15 minutes. Remove the cover and cook for 15 minutes, or until the apples are tender and lightly golden brown.

To prepare the endive: Sauté the endive with the remaining 2 tablespoons of butter for 2 minutes, or until golden brown. Sprinkle with the sugar and add the remaining 3 sage leaves and the stock. Bring the liquid to a simmer, cover, and place in the oven at 350 degrees for 20 minutes, or until the endive is tender. Season to taste with salt and pepper.

ASSEMBLY—Reheat the Red Wine Jus in a small saucepan. Arrange some of the apple rings in the center of each plate and spoon the remaining liquid from the pan around the apple rings. Lay 2 pieces of the endive over the apple rings and arrange some of the duck slices over the endive. Spoon the Red Wine Jus over the duck and around the plates and top with freshly ground black pepper.

WINE NOTES—The minerally, full-bodied flavors of a Puligny-Montrachet seem to balance the apple in the dish, and the rich fruit complements the slightly bitter flavors from the endive. The small producer Verget makes great examples of wines from Puligny that also have enough body to stand up to the duck.

Chapter

12

Beef

POACHED BEEF TENDERLOIN WITH GNOCCHI
AND ROASTED ROOT VEGETABLES

Poached beef tenderloin is indeed a treasure.

It is quite easy to do and the meat literally melts in your mouth like butter. Here the beef is understated, properly balanced with barely browned pieces of gnocchi and chunks of earthy, sweet root vegetables.

And rather than a rich reduction sauce, everything swims in a light, full-flavored beef consommé. Wild mushrooms could be added to make this dish more substantial, but it makes an elegant and satisfying meal with nothing more than a salad of tossed greens. Tuna or salmon work well in place of the beef, and chicken stock can be used in lieu of the consommé.

SERVES 4

3 egg whites, lightly beaten

½ cup chopped onion

½ cup grated carrots

½ cup grated celery

1 cup ground beef

½ cup chopped tomatoes

6 cups Beef Stock (see page 199)

Salt and pepper

1 cup large-diced carrots

1 cup large-diced rutabaga

1 cup large-diced turnips

1 cup plus 1 tablespoon olive oil

1 egg yolk

1 Idaho potato, baked, peeled, and riced

¾ to 1 cup flour

2 teaspoons butter

2 tablespoons lemon juice

1 shallot, minced

1 pound beef tenderloin

METHOD—To prepare the consommé: Whisk together the egg whites, onion, grated carrots, celery, ground beef, and tomato until slightly frothy. Place the Beef Stock in a medium saucepan and whisk the egg white mixture into the stock. Bring the stock to a slow simmer, stirring continuously in a single direction with a wooden spoon. Stir continuously for 15 minutes, or until a raft begins to form. Reduce heat to low, and stop stirring. After the raft forms, break a small hole in it to allow the consommé to come through. Continue to simmer for 45 minutes, or until the liquid is crystal clear. Do not stir. Strain through a fine-mesh sieve lined with cheesecloth, being careful not to break the raft. Discard the raft and season the consommé with salt and pepper.

To prepare the diced vegetables: Place the diced carrots, rutabaga, and turnips in an ovenproof baking pan. Toss with 3 tablespoons of the olive oil and season to taste with salt and pepper. Roast at 375 degrees for 30 to 40 minutes, or until the vegetables are golden brown and tender.

To prepare the gnocchi: Work the egg yolk into the potato and season to taste with salt and pepper. Knead in enough flour so the dough is not sticky. Divide the mixture into 4 portions and roll each portion into a long cigar shape about ½ inch in diameter. Cut the rolls into ½-inch pieces and gently pinch each piece in the center. Refrigerate on a lightly floured sheet pan until ready to

preparing gnocchi

roll into ½ inch
cigar shape

cut & pinch

divide into 4 portions

cook. Poach the gnocchi in boiling salted water for 2 to 3 minutes, or just until they float. Transfer the gnocchi to a large bowl with a slotted spoon. Sauté the gnocchi in the butter over medium heat for 2 to 3 minutes, or until golden brown. Season to taste with salt and pepper.

To prepare the vinaigrette: Whisk together the lemon juice, shallot, and the remaining 6 tablespoons of olive oil and season to taste with salt and pepper.

To prepare the beef: Bring the consommé to a boil. Cut the beef tenderloin into 4 equal pieces lengthwise and place into the consommé. Simmer for 7 minutes, or until the beef is cooked medium-rare. Remove the beef from the consommé, cut each piece into 3 slices, and season the beef with salt and pepper.

ASSEMBLY—Arrange some of the roasted vegetables and the gnocchi in the center of each bowl. Place 3 slices of the beef in each bowl and ladle in the beef consommé. Drizzle the vinaigrette on the beef and around the bowl and top with freshly ground black pepper.

WINE NOTES—Poached beef has a very delicate flavor and rich texture. A full-bodied, fruity Merlot such as Robert Sinskey Vineyards has just enough tannin to cut through the richness and plenty of fruit to complement the flavor of the beef.

MEDITERRANEAN-INSPIRED BEEF TENDERLOIN WITH QUINOA AND RED WINE—BLACK OLIVE VINAIGRETTE

This is great for a luncheon, picnic, or light dinner. The beef, larded with roasted bell pepper, poblanos, eggplant, and anchovies and then grilled, takes on an **especially satisfying and lusty flavor.** It can be cooked hours or even a day or two in advance and sliced when you are ready to serve. The fragrant quinoa and garbanzo bean salad adds substance and chewiness and the red wine—black olive vinaigrette contributes an earthiness that **dramatically grounds all the flavors and textures, simultaneously fusing them together.**

SERVES 4

2 ¼-inch-thick slices eggplant, grilled

1 roasted poblano chile, seeded and cut into batons

1 roasted red bell pepper, seeded and cut into batons

6 anchovies, cleaned

1 pound beef tenderloin, trimmed

Salt and pepper

1 cup plus 2 tablespoons olive oil

1 750-ml bottle red wine

1 cup kalamata olives plus ½ cup of their brine

2½ cups cooked quinoa

1 cup diced cucumbers

¾ cup cooked garbanzo beans

¼ cup chopped fresh parsley

2 tablespoons chopped garlic

1 teaspoon sea salt

METHOD—To lard the beef tenderloin: Cut the eggplant into ¼-inch-wide strips. Using a larding needle, insert the eggplant, poblano, bell pepper, and anchovies into the beef tenderloin horizontally. (If you do not have a larding needle, start from the side of the tenderloin and cut several slits into the tenderloin with a boning knife. Rotate the knife 90 degrees and insert it into the same spots, creating "X's." Using the handle of a wooden spoon, insert the pieces of bell pepper, poblano, eggplant, and anchovy into the slits.) Season the beef tenderloin with salt and pepper and rub with 2 tablespoons of the olive oil. Grill the tenderloin over a moderate flame for 10 to 15 minutes, or until medium-rare. Refrigerate until chilled and cut into 8 slices. Season the meat to taste with salt and pepper.

To prepare the vinaigrette: Simmer the red wine over medium heat for 30 to 40 minutes, or until reduced to ½ cup. Remove from the heat and let cool. Purée the black olives with the brine for 2 minutes. Add the red wine and ¾ cup of the olive oil and purée for 1 minute, or until smooth. Season to taste with salt and pepper.

To prepare the quinoa salad: Toss the quinoa with the cucumbers, garbanzo beans, parsley, and garlic. Fold in the remaining ¼ cup olive oil and season to taste with salt and pepper.

ASSEMBLY—Spoon some of the quinoa salad in the center of each plate and top with 2 of the beef slices. Spoon some of the vinaigrette around the plates and top with freshly ground black pepper and the sea salt.

WINE NOTES—A Cabernet with a hint of bell pepper will accentuate the flavors in this dish. Groth Cabernet Sauvignon from the Napa Valley has very light bell pepper flavors, intense fruit, and a delicate oaky finish that is perfect for the beef.

ZINFANDEL–BRAISED SHORT RIBS WITH MUSTARD SPAETZLE AND AROMATIC VEGETABLES

These short ribs are **succulent and rich, and they are surprisingly simple to prepare.** After marinating overnight, they require nothing more than a slow braising with the vegetables for three to four hours. The ribs can be made well ahead of time and reheated at the last moment. The Zinfandel sauce in this recipe adds a complex fruitiness and acidity that cuts the meat.

Braised greens and tangy mustard spaetzle make this a complete meal— a deeply satisfying meal at that.

SERVES 4

1 cup chopped onions

½ cup chopped leeks

1 Granny Smith apple, chopped

6 cloves garlic, chopped

2 jalapeños, chopped

4 tablespoons canola oil

4 cups Zinfandel

8 short ribs, trimmed of excess fat

5 tablespoons olive oil

4 sprigs thyme

4 sage leaves

1 teaspoon coriander seeds, tied up in cheesecloth to make a sachet

Salt and pepper

4 cups Chicken Stock (see page 201)

2 Yukon Gold potatoes, cut into thick wedges

1 turnip, peeled and cut into thick wedges

⅓ cup chopped raw bacon

4 cups mustard greens, cleaned and chopped

½ cup water

2 tablespoons balsamic vinegar

1 teaspoon sugar

Mustard Spaetzle (recipe follows)

METHOD—To prepare the ribs: Caramelize the onions, leeks, apple, garlic, and jalapeños in a hot sauté pan in 2 tablespoons of the canola oil over medium-high heat for 7 to 10 minutes, or until golden brown. Add the Zinfandel and bring to a simmer. Cool the mixture and add the short ribs, 3 tablespoons olive oil, thyme, sage, and coriander seeds. Cover with plastic wrap and refrigerate for 24 to 36 hours. Remove the ribs from the marinade and season them with salt and pepper. Sear the ribs in a hot roasting pan with the remaining 2 tablespoons canola oil for 2 to 3 minutes on each side, or until golden brown. Add the marinade and stock and cover with aluminum foil. Place the roasting pan in a 350-degree oven and braise for 3 to 4 hours, or until the meat is fork tender.

Cool the ribs in the liquid then remove from the roasting pan and set aside. Strain the liquid and place in a medium saucepan and bring to a simmer. Continue to simmer the braising liquid for 30 to 45 minutes, or until reduced to 1½ cups.

Place the ribs on a roasting pan and reheat in a 350-degree oven for 5 to 10 minutes, or until warm.

To prepare the vegetables: Toss the potato and turnip wedges with the remaining 2 tablespoons olive oil and season to taste with salt and pepper. Place on a sheet pan and roast at 325 degrees for 45 to 60 minutes, or until tender.

To prepare the mustard greens: Render the bacon in a sauté pan and add the mustard greens. Cook for 3 minutes and add the water, balsamic vinegar, and sugar. Continue to cook the greens for 10 to 15 minutes, or until tender, and season to taste with salt and pepper.

ASSEMBLY—Place 2 braised short ribs and some of the mustard greens into each bowl with a small amount of the braising liquid. Arrange some of the roasted potato and turnip wedges in the bowls. Sprinkle with the Mustard Spaetzle and top with freshly ground black pepper.

WINE NOTES—The rich meat from the short ribs melts in your mouth and needs the cleansing quality of tannin to cut through that richness. A red with rich tannin and smoky fruit will be perfect with this dish. A Zinfandel by Steele Vineyards such as Pacini or Catfish vineyards will be a great match.

Mustard Spaetzle

For a more intense mustard flavor, toss the cooked spaetzle,

with a spoonful of grainy mustard.

YIELD: 2 CUPS

2 eggs, beaten

3 tablespoons stone-ground mustard

2 cups flour, or more or less as needed

1¼ cups milk

2 tablespoons butter

Salt and pepper

METHOD—Combine the eggs, mustard, and flour in a medium bowl. Gradually add enough of the milk to make a fairly stiff batter. Cover and refrigerate for 1 hour. Using a pastry bag, spoon, or spaetzle maker, drop ½ teaspoonfuls of batter into simmering, lightly salted water. Cook for about 1 minute, or until the spaetzle floats, and drain. Sauté the spaetzle in the butter for 2 to 3 minutes, or until golden brown and crispy. Season to taste with salt and pepper and keep warm.

STIR-FRIED BEEF WITH BUCKWHEAT NOODLES, TOFU, AND DASHI BROTH

This is a light, clean dish

with a variety of wonderful flavors and textures. And once the vegetables and meat are cut up

and the buckwheat noodles are cooked, it comes together in just minutes.

The dashi broth is remarkably elegant and nourishing, plus it can be prepared up to 2 days in advance.

Mushrooms of any variety can be added for more substance.

Also chiles—such as jalapeños or chipotles—can be added for a boost of heat.

If a richer broth is called for, whisk in a pinch of butter. Finally, duck, tuna,

swordfish, or pork could be substituted for the beef.

SERVES 4

½ cup tamari soy sauce

¼ cup minced ginger

4 tablespoons sesame oil

1 tablespoon garlic chile paste

1 pound beef, cut into 1-inch strips

1 cup diced firm tofu

2 tablespoons sesame seeds

¾ cup diagonally sliced scallions

Salt and pepper

8 ounces buckwheat soba noodles, cooked

2 ounces dried kelp

6 cups Vegetable Stock (see page 220)

¼ cup mirin

2 tablespoons red miso paste

1 tablespoon sugar

3 cups chopped bok choy, blanched

METHOD—To prepare the beef and tofu: Put ¼ cup of the tamari, 2 tablespoons of the ginger, 2 tablespoons sesame oil, and garlic chile paste in a small bowl. Place the beef and tofu into 2 separate bowls, add half of the marinade to each bowl, and marinate for 2 hours.

Stir the sesame seeds into the beef and marinade. In a preheated wok, add the beef mixture and quickly stir-fry for 3 minutes. Add the tofu and stir-fry for 2 minutes. Add the scallions and stir-fry for 1 minute. Remove the mixture from the wok, and season to taste with salt and pepper. Place the buckwheat noodles in the wok and cook for 2 minutes, or until the noodles are warm. Season to taste with salt and pepper.

To prepare the dashi broth: Place the kelp and stock in a sauce pan and simmer for 20 minutes. Remove the kelp from the broth, finely julienne ½ cup of the kelp and add to the noodles, discard the remaining kelp. Add the remaining ¼ cup tamari, 2 tablespoons ginger, the mirin, miso, and sugar to the stock. Simmer the mixture for 20 minutes and season to taste with salt and pepper.

ASSEMBLY—Place some of the noodles and bok choy in the center of each bowl. Top with some of the stir-fry mixture and ladle in some of the dashi broth. Drizzle the remaining 2 tablespoons of sesame oil around the bowl.

WINE NOTES—Carneros Pinot Noirs are a great match for many stir-fry dishes. Their bright fruit tones down the spiciness, and their acidity cleanses the palate. Etude makes a particularly good Pinot Noir that blends with this dish like they were made for each other.

SLOW-BRAISED BEEF STEW WITH CARDAMOM CARROTS AND CHICKPEA PURÉE

This dish is actually done in three parts, but the time it takes to prepare each component is well worth the extra effort. The stew meat is slowly braised with mushrooms and onions until it is supremely tender. The resulting dish has

Middle Eastern overtones

and is far more complex than a typical stew. The haunting flavor of the

cardamom adds a special depth

and a refined intensity normally lacking in such a stew, and the purée of chickpeas, flecked with parsley, provides a silky complement.

Best of all, this dish can be made ahead and reheated as needed.

SERVES 4

1 cup chopped celery

1 cup chopped carrots

2 cups chopped onions

2 tablespoons canola oil

1 bulb garlic, halved

2 portobello mushrooms, cleaned and cut into sixths

12 cremini mushrooms, cleaned

8 scallions, cleaned and cut in half

12 ounces stew meat, cubed

Salt and pepper

4 cups Meat Stock, (see page 208)

6 cloves garlic

1 cup Chicken Stock (see page 201)

1 cup cooked chickpeas

2 tablespoons chopped Italian parsley

12 baby carrots, peeled

1 tablespoon cardamom seeds

2 tablespoons butter

METHOD—To prepare the meat: Place the celery, carrots, and onions in a hot roasting pan with the canola oil and cook for 10 minutes, or until caramelized. Add the garlic, portobello and cremini mushrooms, and the scallions to the pan. Season the beef with salt and pepper and add it to the pan. Cover with the stock and braise in the oven at 325 degrees for 2 to 3 hours, or until the beef is very tender.

To prepare the chickpea purée: Simmer the garlic cloves and Chicken Stock for 20 minutes, or until the cloves are tender. Purée the chickpeas with the Chicken Stock and garlic cloves for 1 minute, or until smooth. Season to taste with salt and pepper and add the chopped Italian parsley.

To prepare the carrots: Place the carrots, cardamom seeds, and butter in a hot sauté pan and cook over medium heat for 5 to 8 minutes, or until the carrots are tender.

ASSEMBLY—Arrange 3 of the carrots in the center of each plate. Spoon some of the beef, mushrooms, and vegetables over the carrots. Spoon the chickpea purée around the plates and top with freshly ground black pepper.

WINE NOTES—This preparation needs a wine with roasted fruit flavors to complement the cardamom. Rioja has plenty of the necessary berry flavor and sweet oak. La Rioja Alto makes a Gran Reserva 904 that is perfect for this dish.

FLANK STEAK WITH CRISPY POLENTA AND
ROASTED SHALLOT VINAIGRETTE

Once the polenta is made (which, for convenience, can be done a day or two ahead of time)

this dish is a snap to put together.

Simply sauté the polenta pieces, grill the flank steak, place them on the plate, and spoon on the

luscious roasted shallot vinaigrette.

and you have a quick and very satisfying plate of food. A mound of sautéed mushrooms, or for something lighter,

asparagus or haricots verts, is a perfect accompaniment.

Crispy potatoes are a splendid substitute for the polenta.

SERVES 4

4 shallots, peeled

1 cup olive oil

3 tablespoons balsamic vinegar

2 tablespoons chopped fresh chives

Salt and pepper

2 tablespoons chopped garlic

¼ cup butter

2 cups cooked polenta, hot

4 4-ounce pieces flank steak

10 sprigs thyme

METHOD—To prepare the vinaigrette: Place the shallots and ¾ cup of the olive oil in a small ovenproof pan and cover tightly. Bake at 350 degrees for 50 to 60 minutes, or until the shallots are soft. Let the shallots cool in the olive oil, and then remove, reserving the oil. Julienne the shallots and put them in a bowl. Add the balsamic vinegar and slowly whisk in the reserved olive oil. Add the chopped chives and season to taste with salt and pepper.

To prepare the polenta: Cook the garlic in 3 tablespoons of butter for 1 minute. Fold into the polenta and season to taste with salt and pepper. Spread the polenta into a ½-inch-thick layer on a small sheet pan. Cover with plastic wrap and refrigerate for 2 hours. Cut the polenta into four 3-inch discs and sauté in the remaining 1 tablespoon butter in a hot, nonstick pan for 2 to 3 minutes on each side, or until golden brown and crispy. Blot on paper towels.

To prepare the steak: Season the steak with salt and pepper and rub with ¼ cup olive oil. Remove the thyme leaves from the stems and rub them onto the beef. Grill for 5 to 7 minutes on each side, or until medium-rare.

ASSEMBLY—Place a piece of the polenta in the center of each plate and top with a piece of the steak. Spoon the Roasted Shallot Vinaigrette over the steak and around the plates and top with freshly ground black pepper.

WINE NOTES—The warm garlic flavors in the polenta mesh beautifully with Italian varietals. The rich fruit of Barbera d'Alba from a producer like Giacomo Conterno beautifully balances the garlic, and has the full acidity needed for the shallot vinaigrette.

Chapter

13

Dessert

PINEAPPLE–POLENTA UPSIDE–DOWN CAKE WITH MANGO AND CARAMEL–LIME ICE CREAM

This dessert is great right out of the oven or at room temperature, so it can be made hours or even a day or two ahead. The lightly caramelized pineapple slices are elegantly contrasted by the soul-satisfying yet light polenta cake. The mango slices lend the dessert a cleansing freshness, and the caramel ice cream adds richness. Apples, pears, slightly underripe peaches, or any fruit that retains some of its body and texture after cooking would work well in place of the pineapple.

SERVES 10

¾ cup butter

2¼ cups sugar

3 eggs

6 egg yolks

¾ cup plus 1 tablespoon flour

½ cup plus 2 tablespoons uncooked polenta

¾ teaspoon baking powder

½ teaspoon salt

½ cup water

10 ⅛-inch-thick round pineapple slices

Pulp of ½ vanilla bean

1 cup julienned mango

¼ cup ground Macadamia Nut Praline (see page 209, Nut Praline)

Caramel-Lime Ice Cream (recipe follows)

Oven-Dried Pineapple Chips (recipe follows)

METHOD—To make the cake: Cream the butter and 1 cup of the sugar. Add the eggs and egg yolks one at a time, mixing thoroughly after each addition. Combine the flour, polenta, baking powder, and salt in a separate bowl and add to the batter, mixing completely.

Cook ¾ cup of the sugar and ¼ cup of the water in a small, heavy-bottomed sauté pan over medium heat for 10 minutes, or until golden brown and caramelized. Wrap the bottoms of ten 2½-inch-diameter by 1½-inch-high ring molds with aluminum foil, lightly oil the inside of the rings, and place them on a sheet pan. Pour in and swirl around just enough of the caramelized sugar to cover the bottom of each mold.

Remove the core from each pineapple slice with a ½-inch-diameter ring cutter and trim the pineapple slice with a 2½-inch-diameter ring cutter so the pineapple slices fit tightly in the bottom of the ring molds. Press the pineapple rings into the molds and refrigerate for 5 minutes. Spoon in the batter to

spoon in batter

fill the molds three-quarters of the way full. Bake at 350 degrees for 20 minutes, or until the cake springs back when pressed lightly in the center. Invert the cakes on the sheet pan while warm and remove the foil and the ring mold.

To prepare the mangoes: Place the remaining ½ cup sugar, ¼ cup water, and the vanilla pulp in a medium sauté pan and bring to a simmer. Add the mango and cook for 2 minutes, or until the mango is just warmed through.

ASSEMBLY—Place some of the mango and the cooking liquid in the center of each plate and top with a cake. Sprinkle the Macadamia Nut Praline on the cake and around the plate. Place a scoop of the Caramel-Lime Ice Cream on top of each cake and insert an Oven-Dried Pineapple Chip upright in the ice cream.

WINE NOTES—The intense sweetness of the pineapple in this dish can only be balanced by a sweeter wine. The orange blossom and tropical fruit aromas of the Muskat Ottonel Beerenauslese from Alois Kracher is a great balance for the sweetness as well as having a cleansing acidity to overcome the sweetness of the wine and dessert.

Caramel-Lime Ice Cream

Chopped pecans or chocolate pieces make a nice addition to this ice cream.

YIELD: ABOUT 3 CUPS

2 cups heavy cream

1 teaspoon lime zest

¾ cup sugar

4 egg yolks

3 tablespoons freshly squeezed lime juice

METHOD—Prepare an ice water bath.

Bring the cream and lime zest to a boil, remove from heat, and cover. Cook the sugar in a medium saucepan over medium heat for 5 to 7 minutes, or until golden brown and all the sugar is dissolved. Add the hot cream to the sugar and stir until completely combined. Whisk the egg yolks and pour in some of the hot cream to temper the eggs. Pour the egg mixture into the cream and cook for 2 to 3 minutes, or until the mixture coats the back of a spoon and steam rises from the surface. Strain through a fine-mesh sieve and cool over the ice water bath, stirring occasionally, until chilled.

Add the lime juice to the cooled cream mixture and freeze in an ice cream machine. Keep frozen until ready to use.

Oven-Dried Pineapple Chips

Try this with apple, strawberry, or banana slices.

YIELD: 10 CHIPS

10 ¹⁄₁₆-inch-thick pineapple wedges

2 teaspoons sugar

METHOD—Lay the pineapple slices on a non-stick sheet pan and sprinkle lightly with the sugar. Bake at 225 degrees for 75 to 90 minutes, or until dry and light golden brown. Remove the pineapple from the pan while warm, set aside to cool completely, and store in an airtight container at room temperature until ready to use or up to 2 days.

CHOCOLATE-GINGER TRUFFLE TART WITH PEAR-CARAMEL SAUCE

This is what you might call an *"adult"* chocolate dessert.

It's intense, certainly, but notes of ginger and pear provide refined flavors that simultaneously tame the chocolate and highlight it.

A cookielike chocolate tart shell adds a delightful and delicate texture.

And an almost regal Pear-Caramel Sauce offers a simple,

fruity sweetness that reels in the chocolate,

toning down its bittersweet flavor. With just a few simple adjustments, this could become a white chocolate tart

or converted from a large tart to smaller individual servings.

SERVES 8

½ cup plus 1 tablespoon butter

½ cup sugar

¾ teaspoon pure vanilla extract

½ teaspoon salt

⅓ cup sifted unsweetened cocoa powder, plus additional for dusting

1 cup flour

12 ounces bittersweet chocolate, chopped

1 cup heavy cream

½ cup peeled, chopped fresh ginger

½ cup plus 2 tablespoons Preserved Ginger (see page 211)

Pear-Caramel Sauce (see page 210)

½ cup ground Pecan Praline (see page 209, Nut Praline)

METHOD—To make the tart dough: Cream ½ cup of the butter, the sugar, vanilla, and salt until smooth. Add the cocoa powder and mix well. Add the flour and mix until incorporated. Transfer the dough to a lightly floured work surface and shape it into a ball. Cover with plastic wrap and refrigerate for 1 hour.

Roll out the dough to ⅛-inch thick on the lightly floured work surface. Line the inside of a 9-inch-diameter tart pan with the dough, discarding any extra dough that hangs over the sides of the pan. Prick the dough with a fork and bake at 375 degrees for 15 to 20 minutes, or until the crust is set around the edges. Cool completely and remove from the pan.

To make the truffle filling: Place the chocolate and the remaining 1 tablespoon butter in a medium bowl. Bring the cream and fresh ginger to a boil, strain the mixture over the chocolate, and discard the ginger. Let the chocolate mixture stand for 3 minutes and then whisk until smooth. Fold in ½ cup of Preserved Ginger. Pour the mixture into the tart shell and refrigerate for 3 hours.

ASSEMBLY—Dust the tart with cocoa powder and cut into 8 slices. Place 1 slice in the center of each plate and spoon the Pear-Caramel Sauce around the slices. Sprinkle the Pecan Praline and remaining preserved Ginger around the plates.

WINE NOTES—Ginger is complemented by the delicate spice flavors of a younger style of Tawny Port. Graham's 10-year-old tawny still has much of its original fruit, making it perfect for the chocolate, and enough acidity to pair well with the Pear-Caramel Sauce.

BING CHERRY—BROWNIE SUNDAE WITH
BITTERSWEET CHOCOLATE—KONA COFFEE SAUCE

This dessert should **bring chocolate lovers to their knees.**

Plus, it's easy to make, primarily because all the components can be prepared in advance

and assembled at the last moment.

The result is creaminess, crunchiness, chewiness, fruitiness, and intense

chocolate all melting decadently together.

If you want to heighten the effect, serve the brownie warm

and substitute bittersweet chocolate ice cream for the vanilla.

SERVES 8 TO 12

¾ cup sugar

1 cup thinly sliced fresh pineapple

1 cup heavy cream

½ teaspoon ground cinnamon

1½ cups Bing cherries,
pitted and quartered

½ cup Vanilla Simple Syrup
(see page 219)

2 baby bananas, peeled and quartered

Bittersweet Chocolate–Bing Cherry
Brownies (recipe follows)

Bittersweet Chocolate–Kona Coffee
Sauce (see page 199)

¾ cup chopped Hazelnut Praline
(see page 209, Nut Praline)

Vanilla Bean Ice Cream
(recipe follows)

METHOD—To make the pineapple sauce: Cook ½ cup of the sugar in a small, heavy-bottomed sauté pan over medium-low heat for 6 to 7 minutes, or until golden brown and caramelized. Add the pineapple and cook for 5 minutes, or until the pineapple is hot.

To make the cinnamon cream: Whip the cream and cinnamon until doubled in volume. Add 2 tablespoons of the sugar and whip until stiff peaks form.

To prepare the cherries: Warm the cherries in the Vanilla Simple Syrup over medium heat for 3 minutes, or until just warm.

To prepare the bananas: Sprinkle the banana quarters with the remaining 2 tablespoons sugar and caramelize with a small blowtorch.

ASSEMBLY—Spoon some of the cinnamon cream in the center of each plate. Place a brownie on top of the cream and arrange 2 of the caramelized banana quarters on opposite sides of the brownie. Drizzle the Bittersweet Chocolate–Kona Coffee Sauce on the brownie and around the plate. Spoon the warm cherries and their juices over the brownies. Spoon the pineapple sauce and pineapple around the plate. Sprinkle the praline over the cherries and around the plates and top with a scoop of the Vanilla Bean Ice Cream.

WINE NOTES—The light spice flavors and rich fruit of a late-bottled vintage port, such as Taylor Fladgate, blend beautifully with the cherries in this dessert. The delicate oak flavors in the port enhance the flavors of the coffee in the sauce.

Bittersweet Chocolate–Bing Cherry Brownies

This is a great, intense chocolate treat all on its own.

YIELD: ABOUT 16 BROWNIES

2 eggs

½ teaspoon pure vanilla extract

1 cup sugar

½ pound bittersweet chocolate, chopped

½ cup butter

½ cup flour

¼ cup unsweetened cocoa powder

1 cup Bing cherries, pitted and quartered

METHOD—Whisk together the eggs, vanilla, and sugar until smooth. Slowly melt the chocolate and butter in the top of a double boiler. Add the melted chocolate to the egg mixture and whisk until incorporated. Sift together the flour and cocoa and fold into the mixture. Fold in the cherries. Spread the batter into a parchment-lined 8-inch square pan and bake at 350 degrees for 20 to 25 minutes, or until just done. Let cool in the pan and cut into 2-inch squares.

Vanilla Bean Ice Cream

If you can't locate a fresh vanilla bean, try using a splash of a high-quality pure vanilla extract.

YIELD: APPROXIMATELY 3 CUPS

2 cups heavy cream

Pulp and pod of 1 vanilla bean

4 egg yolks

6 tablespoons sugar

METHOD—Prepare an ice water bath.

Bring the cream and vanilla pulp and bean to a boil. Whisk together the egg yolks and sugar in a bowl and slowly pour in some of the hot cream to temper the eggs. Pour the egg mixture into the cream mixture and cook for 2 to 3 minutes, or until the mixture coats the back of a spoon and steam rises from the surface. Strain through a fine-mesh sieve and cool over the ice water bath, stirring occasionally, until chilled. Freeze in an ice cream machine and keep frozen until ready to use.

CARAMELIZED APPLE, PUMPKIN, AND PECAN STRUDEL WITH GINGER—MAPLE SYRUP ICE CREAM

This type of strudel, while not totally authentic, is quite delicious and very versatile in terms of the ingrdients that can be used in the filling. Here, pumpkin has been chosennot only for its sweetness and slight starchiness, but also for its sating, melt-away texture. Pecans or hazelnuts provide a crunchiness and richness that round out the depth of flavor. The ginger-maple ice cream ensures the dessert finishes with soothing, autumn overtones. The strudel can be made a few hours in advance and baked right before serving.

SERVES 6

¾ cup plus 5 tablespoons granulated sugar

Pulp of 1 vanilla bean

3 cups peeled and thinly sliced Granny Smith apples

1 cup diced raw pumpkin

¼ cup water

1 teaspoon ground cinnamon

½ teaspoon ground nutmeg

1 cup puréed cooked pumpkin

4 sheets filo dough

½ cup melted butter

1 cup chopped pecans

Cinnamon-Butterscotch Sauce (see page 202)

Ginger–Maple Syrup Ice Cream (recipe follows)

4 teaspoons chiffonade-cut mint

4 teaspoons Mint Syrup (see page 209)

METHOD—To prepare the apples: Cook ½ cup of the granulated sugar and the vanilla bean pulp in a medium, heavy-bottomed sauté pan over medium-low heat for 5 to 8 minutes, or until golden brown and caramelized. Add the apples and cook for 10 minutes, or until the apple slices are tender. Remove the apples from the pan with a slotted spoon and let cool to room temperature.

To prepare the diced pumpkin: Place the raw pumpkin in the pan with the liquid from the apples and cook over medium heat for 7 to 10 minutes, or until the pumpkin is cooked. Let cool to room temperature.

To prepare the pumpkin purée: Cook ¼ cup of the sugar, the water, cinnamon, and nutmeg in a medium, heavy-bottomed sauté pan for 5 minutes, or until the sugar is dissolved. Add the puréed pumpkin and stir until smooth. Remove from the heat and cool to room temperature.

To prepare the strudel: Place a sheet of filo on a work surface, brush lightly with the melted butter, and sprinkle lightly with 1 tablespoon of the sugar, and repeat the process until there are 3 layers of filo. Cover with a final layer of filo, brush lightly with the melted butter, and set aside at room temperature.

Spread the pumpkin purée on the filo stack and lay the apple slices over the pumpkin purée. Sprinkle with the chopped pecans and gently roll the filo strudel into a log shape. Brush with melted butter and sprinkle with the remaining 2 tablespoons sugar. Cut the log in half and place on a parchment-lined sheet pan. Bake at 375 degrees for 40 to 50 minutes, or until the filo is golden brown and crispy. Let cool slightly and cut each strudel into 6 diagonal pieces.

ASSEMBLY—Place the Cinnamon-Butterscotch Sauce in a small pan over low heat for 5 minutes, or until just warm. Place 2 pieces of the strudel in the center of each plate and spoon some of the Cinnamon-Butterscotch Sauce around the plates. Spoon some of the diced pumpkin and the juices around the plates and top with a scoop of the Ginger–Maple Syrup Ice Cream. Sprinkle the mint and drizzle the Mint Syrup around the ice cream.

WINE NOTES—The warm almost autumnal flavors of the dish need a wine with sweetness and spice. Chambers "Rutherglen" Muscat is a liqueur style from Australia that is aged in a manner similar to a tawny port. It has a delicate spice and richness of fruit that is wonderful with the strudel.

Ginger–Maple Syrup Ice Cream

Try swirling some maple syrup into the finished ice cream.

YIELD: ABOUT 1 QUART

3 cups heavy cream
½ cup peeled, chopped fresh ginger
6 egg yolks
1 cup pure maple syrup

METHOD—Prepare an ice water bath.

Bring the cream and ginger to a boil in a medium saucepan. Strain through a fine-mesh sieve and discard the ginger. Whisk together the egg yolks and maple syrup and slowly pour in some of the hot cream mixture to temper the eggs. Pour the egg yolk mixture into the cream mixture and cook over medium-low heat for 2 minutes, stirring continuously. Strain through a fine-mesh sieve and immediately cool over the ice water bath. Freeze in an ice cream machine and keep frozen until ready to use.

BURNT CARAMEL—ARBORIO RICE CRÈME BRÛLÉE

This dessert is a cross between a rice pudding and a crème brûlée.

It is as satisfying as it is delicate,

and the burnt caramel flavor makes the concoction utterly sensual. An interesting variation

would be maple syrup or a blood orange caramel in place of the burnt caramel flavor.

Also, pieces of banana or peach could be added to each brûlée mold right before baking. With these adjustments,

the brûlée becomes more substantial and assumes a cleansing fruitiness.

Finally, for convenience, the brûlée can be made a day ahead

and glazed right before serving.

SERVES 6

1 cup sugar

1½ cups heavy cream

2 eggs

2 egg yolks

½ cup arborio rice

1 cup water

1 cup milk

¼ cup brandy

½ cup dried black currants

Sugar, for dusting

METHOD—To make the crème brûlée: Prepare an ice water bath. Cook the sugar in a small, heavy-bottomed sauté pan for 5 minutes, or until dark brown and caramelized. Add the cream and cook until the mixture is smooth. Whisk together the eggs and egg yolks, and slowly pour in some of the hot cream. Pour the eggs into the cream mixture and cool over the ice water bath.

Simmer the arborio rice and water over medium heat, stirring frequently, for 20 minutes, or until all of the liquid is absorbed. Add ½ cup of the milk and simmer until all of the liquid is absorbed. Add the remaining ½ cup milk and cook until all of the liquid is absorbed.

Cook the brandy and currants for 3 to 4 minutes, or until most of the liquid is absorbed. Fold the currants and any liquid into the arborio rice.

Place some of the arborio rice in the bottom of six 4-to 5-ounce crème brûlée molds. Pour the cream and egg mixture over the rice and bake in a water bath at 300 degrees for 25 minutes, or until the custard is set.

Refrigerate the custard for 1 hour, or until completely cool.

ASSEMBLY—Sprinkle an even, heavy dusting of sugar over the top of the custard and caramelize the sugar with a small blowtorch until the sugar melts and turns golden brown.

WINE NOTES—The rich caramel flavors of Madeira are the perfect companion to the caramel flavors of the crème brûlée. A rich, young style like Blandy's 10-year-old malmsey is a wonderful complement to this dessert.

TROPICAL FRUIT—MACADAMIA NUT NAPOLEON

This napoleon is whimsical and absolutely open to interpretation.
Practically any type or combination of seasonal fruit can be used. The flavors of the vanilla, macadamia nuts, and tropical fruits
all dance with sensuality that will appeal to any palate. Plump, luscious fruit slices blend
into the satiny coconut cream, which in turn is offset
by the crispy vanilla–macadamia nut tuiles and the crunchy macadamia nut brittle.
This utterly joyous dessert can be easily assembled in any size—for instance just a petite tart is the perfect
precursor to a slice of intense chocolate cake.

SERVES 6

1 cup Vanilla Simple Syrup
(see page 219)

1 tablespoon freshly squeezed
lime juice

1 cup peeled and thinly sliced mango

½ cup peeled and thinly sliced papaya

½ cup peeled and thinly
sliced pineapple

½ cup peeled and thinly sliced guava

¼ cup heavy cream

½ cup mascarpone

2 tablespoons sugar

Vanilla–Macadamia Nut Tuiles
(recipe follows)

½ cup chopped Macadamia Nut
Praline (see page 209, Nut Praline)

¼ cup toasted coconut

METHOD—To prepare the fruit: Cook the Vanilla Simple Syrup, the lime juice, ½ cup of the sliced mango, and all of the papaya, pineapple, and guava over medium heat for 5 to 8 minutes, or until the fruits are warmed through. Pour most of the liquid from the pan into a blender and purée with the remaining ½ cup of mango for 1 minute, or until smooth. Refrigerate the fruit and the sauce for 30 minutes, or until chilled.

To make the cream: Whip the heavy cream, mascarpone, and sugar with an electric mixer on high speed until medium stiff peaks form.

ASSEMBLY—Place 1 teaspoon of the mascarpone cream in the center of each plate. Place a tuile over the cream and place 2 teaspoons of the cream in the center of the tuile. Spoon some of the warm fruit over the cream and sprinkle with the chopped praline. Continue to layer with the cream, fruit, praline, and tuiles until you have 3 layers of fruit and 4 layers of tuiles. Spoon some of the mango purée around the plate and sprinkle with the toasted coconut.

WINE NOTES—The nut and fruit elements in this napoleon suggest nut and caramel flavors in wine choice. An older Malmsey Madeira, such as a 15-or 20-year-old from Blandy's, fit the bill. Older tawny ports will also blend just as well.

tropical fruit

vanilla macadamia nut tuiles

mascarpone cream

mango puree

Vanilla–Macadamia Nut Tuiles

These tuiles can be made in a variety of shapes.

YIELD: ABOUT 40 TUILES

¼ cup sugar

¼ cup plus 1 tablespoon flour

Pulp of ½ vanilla bean

¼ cup plus 1 tablespoon butter, melted and cooled to room temperature

3 egg whites

¼ cup ground macadamia nuts

METHOD—Combine the sugar and flour in a small bowl. Add the vanilla pulp, melted butter, and egg whites and stir until smooth.

Cut a 2½-inch square in the center of a piece of cardboard or heavy plastic to create a template. Place the template on a Silpat-lined sheet pan, and spread a thin layer of the tuile batter in the template. Remove the template and repeat the process until you have at least 24 tuiles. Sprinkle the tuiles with the macadamia nuts and bake at 300 degrees for 8 to 12 minutes, or until golden brown.

Remove the tuiles from the sheet pan while warm and store in an airtight container at room temperature until needed or up to 1 day.

Chapter 14

Pantry

*Apricot Curry Sauce

This sauce would be

a nice accompaniment to pork.

YIELD: 2½ CUPS

¾ cup dried apricots

1½ teaspoons hot curry powder

½ cup rice wine vinegar

1 cup water

METHOD—Purée all of the ingredients for 3 minutes, or until smooth. Refrigerate overnight and strain through a fine-mesh sieve. Refrigerate until ready to use or for up to 1 week.

Basil Oil

Try this oil

with a piece of sourdough bread.

YIELD: 1½ CUPS

½ cup firmly packed fresh basil

½ cup fresh spinach leaves

¼ cup fresh flat-leaf parsley

¼ cup olive oil

1 cup canola oil

METHOD—Blanch the basil, spinach, and parsley in boiling salted water for 45 seconds and immediately shock in ice water. Squeeze out the excess water, coarsely chop, and then purée with the olive and canola oils for 3 to 5 minutes, or until bright green. Pour the mixture into a container, cover, and refrigerate overnight.

Strain the oil through a fine-mesh sieve and discard the solids. Refrigerate for an additional 24 hours and decant. Keep refrigerated until ready to use or for up to 1 week.

Beef Stock

You can reduce this stock even more for a richer flavor.

YIELD: 2 QUARTS

6 pounds beef bones

2 cups chopped carrots

2 cups chopped celery

4 cups chopped onions

3 cloves garlic, peeled

2 tablespoons canola oil

½ cup chopped tomato

2 cups red wine

1 bay leaf

1 tablespoon whole black peppercorns

METHOD—Place the bones in a roasting pan and bake at 450 degrees for 1 hour, or until they are golden brown. Turn the bones after 30 minutes to ensure even browning.

Sauté the carrots, celery, onion, and garlic in a large stock pot over medium-high heat for 7 minutes, or until caramelized. Add the tomato and cook for 2 minutes. Deglaze the pan with the red wine and cook until most of the wine is cooked out. Add the browned bones, bay leaf, and peppercorns and cover with water. Bring to a boil and reduce the heat. Slowly simmer for 6 to 8 hours or until reduced to 2 quarts, periodically skimming the impurities that rise to the surface. Strain through a fine-mesh sieve.

*Bittersweet Chocolate–Kona Coffee Sauce

When this sauce is chilled it can be scooped into balls and dusted with cocoa to make truffles.

YIELD: ABOUT 2 CUPS

1 cup heavy cream

¼ ounce espresso-grind kona coffee

¼ cup sugar

7 ounces bittersweet chocolate, chopped

METHOD—Place the cream, espresso, and sugar in a saucepan and bring to a simmer. Add the chocolate, remove from the heat, and stir until smooth. Serve immediately, or refrigerate for up to 1 week and warm before serving.

*Black Olive–Caper Vinaigrette

If you reduce the oil in this recipe to 2 tablespoons it makes

a great tapenade.

YIELD: ABOUT 1 CUP

3 tablespoons balsamic vinegar

1/2 cup plus 1 tablespoon olive oil

2 tablespoons minced shallots

1/2 cup pitted and quartered kalamata olives

1/4 cup capers

Salt and pepper

METHOD—Whisk together the vinegar and olive oil and add the shallots. Finely chop the olives and the capers, add to the bowl, and season to taste with salt and pepper.

*Black Pepper–Vanilla Bean Vinaigrette

Try this with grilled shrimp or lobster.

YIELD: 1 CUP

1 tablespoon freshly squeezed lemon juice

1 tablespoon freshly squeezed orange juice

3 tablespoons rice wine vinegar

Pulp of 1 vanilla bean

1 teaspoon freshly ground black pepper

1/2 cup canola oil

1/4 cup olive oil

METHOD—Combine the lemon juice, orange juice, vinegar, vanilla, and black pepper in a small bowl. Slowly whisk in the canola and olive oils. Serve immediately or refrigerate for up to 3 days.

Brioche

Brioche is best right out of the oven, but keeping a loaf in the freezer is great for when you're in a pinch.

YIELD: ONE 9 BY 4-INCH LOAF

1/4 cup milk, warmed

2 teaspoons active dry yeast

1/2 cup plus 3 1/2 tablespoons all-purpose flour

1 1/2 cups plus 3 tablespoons high-gluten flour

2 tablespoons plus 1/2 teaspoon sugar

1 teaspoon salt

2 eggs

3/4 cup butter, at room temperature

METHOD—Pour the milk over the yeast in a small bowl and let sit for several minutes. Stir to dissolve the yeast. Combine the flours, sugar, and salt in a large mixing bowl, add the milk and eggs, and mix in an electric mixer fitted with a dough hook on low speed until the dough comes together. Add the butter and continue to mix for 25 to 30 minutes, scraping occasionally, or until the dough is smooth and pulls away from the sides of the bowl.

Place the dough in an oiled bowl and cover with plastic wrap. Let rise in a warm place for 2 hours, or until the dough has doubled in size. Punch down the dough and place into a buttered, floured loaf pan. Cover and let rise in a warm place for 1 hour. Bake at 375 degrees for 35 to 45 minutes, or until golden brown. Remove from the oven and cool on a wire rack.

Chicken Stock

You can make a large batch of stock, freeze it in ice cube trays, and store it in resealable bags the freezer.

YIELD: 2 QUARTS

6 pounds chicken bones

3 cups chopped onions

2 cups chopped carrots

2 cups chopped celery

1 cup chopped leeks

1 tablespoon white peppercorns

1 bay leaf

METHOD—Place all of the ingredients in a large stockpot and cover three-quarters of the way with cold water. Bring to a boil, reduce the heat to low, and slowly simmer uncovered for 4 hours, skimming every 30 minutes to remove impurities that rise to the surface. Strain, discard the solids, and cook over medium heat for 30 to 45 minutes, or until reduced to 2 quarts. Store in the refrigerator for up to 2 days or freeze for up to 2 months.

Cinnamon-Butterscotch Sauce

This is great with a warm slice of apple pie or vanilla ice cream.

YIELD: ABOUT 2 CUPS

¾ cup firmly packed brown sugar

1 cup heavy cream

2 drops cinnamon oil

½ cup butter

1 stick cinnamon

METHOD—Place all of the ingredients in a large saucepan and cook over medium heat for 30 minutes, whisking occasionally. Remove and discard the cinnamon stick. Serve immediately or refrigerate for up to 1 week.

Curry Oil

You can use sweet or hot curry in this recipe depending on your tastes.

YIELD: ½ CUP

½ cup chopped onion

¾ cup canola oil

2 tablespoons curry powder

METHOD—Sauté the onion in 2 tablespoons of the canola oil over medium heat for 5 minutes, or until translucent. Add the curry powder and cook for 3 minutes. Purée the mixture with the remaining ½ cup plus 1 tablespoon canola oil for 3 minutes, or until completely combined. Refrigerate for 1 day then strain through a fine-mesh sieve. Let stand for 3 more hours and carefully decant.

Dill Oil

Try a drizzle over a piece of

sautéed salmon.

YIELD: 1 CUP

2 cups fresh dill

1½ cups canola oil

½ cup olive oil

METHOD—Blanch the dill in boiling salted water for 15 seconds. Immediately shock in ice water and drain. Squeeze out the excess water. Purée with the canola and olive oils for 3 to 4 minutes, or until bright green. Pour into a container, cover, and refrigerate overnight.

Strain the oil through a fine-mesh sieve and discard the solids. Refrigerate for an additional 24 hours and decant. Refrigerate until needed.

Duck Confit

Try shredding the meat and stuffing a

crepe for an appetizer.

YIELD: 4 LEGS AND THIGHS

6 tablespoons kosher salt

1 tablespoon sugar

1 tablespoon coarsely ground black pepper

1 tablespoon sliced garlic

2 teaspoons peeled, chopped, fresh ginger

4 duck legs with thighs attached

2½ cups rendered duck fat

METHOD—Combine the salt, sugar, pepper, garlic, and ginger in a small bowl. Rub the duck legs with the mixture, pack tightly in a small container, and cover with plastic wrap. Refrigerate for 24 hours, turning the pieces over after 12 hours.

Rinse the duck legs and place in a heavy-bottomed pot. Cover with the duck fat and cover with a lid. Bake at 225 degrees for 6 hours, or until the meat is fork tender. Cool the duck in the fat and store in the refrigerator for up to 2 weeks. When ready to use, remove the duck from the fat, place skin side down in a very hot sauté pan, and cook for 5 minutes to crisp up the skin. (It may need to be put in the oven for a few minutes to warm it through.) Once the skin is crispy, remove the leg and thigh bones, leaving the meat intact.

Duck Jus

Meat or beef jus could be used in lieu of the duck jus, or you can reduce it down for a thicker sauce.

YIELD: 1½ CUPS

3 pounds duck bones

1 cup chopped carrots

1 cup chopped celery

1 cup chopped onions

3 cloves garlic

2 tablespoons canola oil

½ cup chopped tomato

2 cups red wine

1 bay leaf

1 tablespoon whole black peppercorns

METHOD—Place the bones in a roasting pan and bake at 450 degrees for 30 to 45 minutes, or until they are golden-brown. Turn the bones after 20 minutes to ensure even browning. In a large stockpot, sauté the carrots, celery, onions, and garlic in the canola oil over high heat for 7 minutes, or until caramelized. Add the tomato and pour in the red wine to deglaze the pan. Continue to cook until most of the wine is cooked out. Add the bones, bay leaf, and peppercorns, and cover with cold water. Bring to a boil, reduce the heat to low, and slowly simmer for 4 hours. Strain, and reduce the stock to 1½ cups, periodically skimming away the impurities that rise to the surface. Strain the duck jus through a fine-mesh sieve.

*Gingered Mustard Sauternes Sauce

You can add a spoonful of honey if a sweeter sauce is desired.

YIELD: 3 CUPS

4 cups sauternes, reduced to 2 cups

3¾ ounces whole-grain mustard

¼ cup Preserved Ginger, chopped (see page 211)

½ cup butter

2 tablespoons rice wine vinegar

Salt and pepper

METHOD—Whisk together all the ingredients and season to taste with salt and pepper.

*Ginger-Soy-Hijiki Sauce

This sauce is great tossed with buckwheat soba noodles.

YIELD: 1½ CUPS

¼ ounce dried hijiki seaweed

2 tablespoons water

½ tablespoon finely diced jalepeño

½ shallot, finely diced

½ cup minced ginger

1 teaspoon minced garlic

1 teaspoon olive oil

2 tablespoons rice wine vinegar

3 tablespoons mirin

5½ tablespoons tamari

2 tablespoons sesame oil

½ cup mayonnaise

METHOD—Soak the hijiki in the water for 30 minutes and drain. Sauté the jalepeño, shallot, ginger, and garlic in the olive oil over medium heat for 1 minute. Remove from the pan and place in a bowl. Add the vinegar, mirin, tamari, and hijiki and slowly whisk in the sesame oil. Let cool and purée with the mayonnaise until smooth.

Hamhock-Flavored White Navy Beans

Bacon can be used instead of the hamhocks in this recipe.

YIELD: ABOUT 3 CUPS

1½ cup white navy beans, soaked overnight in water

¾ cup diced hamhock

METHOD—Place the beans and hamhock in a samll saucepan and add enough water to cover the beans. Cook over medium low heat for 1½ to 2 hours, or until extremely tender. (Additional water may be needed during cooking.) Remove from the heat and drain.

Herb Oil

Herb oils can be made with any type of herb, such as basil, dill, or tarragon.

YIELD: ½ CUP

1 cup fresh chives
1 cup fresh flat-leaf parsley
1 cup watercress
1 cup canola oil

METHOD—Blanch the chives, parsley, and watercress in boiling salted water for 20 seconds and immediately shock in ice water to stop the cooking process. Drain the water, squeeze out any excess liquid, and coarsely chop the herbs. Purée the herbs with the canola oil for 3 to 4 minutes, or until the mixture is bright green, and refrigerate overnight. Strain through a fine-mesh sieve and discard the solids. Refrigerate for 24 hours and then decant the oil. The oil may be stored in the refrigerator for up to 1 month.

Hot and Sour Cucumbers

These cucumbers hold in the refrigerator for up to 1 week. For spicier cucumbers, add a minced habanero chile pepper.

YIELD: ABOUT 3 CUPS

2 cucumbers, cut in half lengthwise
1½ bay leaves
1½ cups rice wine vinegar
1 cup sugar
1 jalepeño, chopped
6 ounces thinly sliced red onion
3 ounces thinly sliced fennel
½ tablespoon crushed pink peppercorns

METHOD—Scrape the seeds from the cucumbers, discard the seeds, and thinly slice the cucumber. Place the bay leaves, vinegar, sugar, and jalepeño in a saucepan and simmer for 5 minutes. Strain and cool. Combine the cucumbers, onion, fennel, peppercorns, and cooled vinegar mixture and refrigerate for at least 3 hours.

Meat Stock

YIELD: 2 QUARTS

6 pounds beef, lamb,
or venison bones

2 cups chopped carrots

2 cups chopped celery

4 cups chopped onions

3 cloves garlic

2 tablespoons canola oil

$\frac{1}{2}$ cup chopped tomatoes

2 cups red wine

1 bay leaf

1 tablespoon black peppercorns

METHOD—Place the bones in a roasting pan and bake at 450 degrees for 1 hour, or until golden brown. Turn the bones after 30 minutes to ensure even browning.

In a large stockpot, sauté the carrots, celery, onions, and garlic in the oil over medium-high heat for 7 minutes, or until caramelized. Add the tomatoes and cook for 2 minutes. Deglaze the pan with the red wine and cook until most of the wine is cooked out. Add the browned bones, bay leaf, and peppercorns, cover with water, and bring to a boil. Reduce the heat and slowly simmer for 6 to 8 hours, or until reduced to 2 quarts, periodically skimming and discarding the impurities that rise to the surface. Strain through a fine-mesh sieve. Keep in the refrigerator for up to 2 days or freeze for up to 2 months.

Meat Stock Reduction

YIELD: 1$\frac{1}{2}$ CUPS

2 cups chopped Spanish onions

1 cup chopped carrots

1 cup chopped celery

2 tablespoons canola oil

1 cup red wine

1$\frac{1}{2}$ quarts Meat Stock
(see above)

4 sprigs thyme

METHOD—Caramelize the vegetables in the canola oil in a medium saucepan over high heat for 10 minutes, or until golden brown. Add the red wine to deglaze the pan and cook until most of the red wine has cooked away. Add the Meat Stock and simmer for 1 hour. Strain, return to the saucepan with the thyme, and simmer for 5 minutes. Remove the thyme and simmer for about 30 minutes, or until reduced to about 1$\frac{1}{2}$ cups. Strain through a fine-mesh sieve.

Mint Syrup

This syrup is also great made from basil or lemon balm.

YIELD: APPROXIMATELY ⅓ CUP

½ cup fresh mint leaves
¼ cup fresh spinach leaves
¼ cup Simple Syrup (see page 215)
1 tablespoon oil

METHOD—Blanch the mint and spinach in boiling water for 10 seconds, remove from the pan, and immediately shock in ice water. Squeeze out the excess water and coarsely chop. Purée with the Simple Syrup and oil for 3 minutes and strain through a fine-mesh sieve. Refrigerate until needed.

Nut Praline

Praline can be coarsely chopped or finely ground, depending on the desired use.

YIELD: 1 CUP

½ cup sugar
¼ cup water
½ cup toasted macadamia nuts, pecans, or hazelnuts

METHOD—In a medium, heavy-bottomed sauté pan, combine the sugar and water over medium heat and cook for 10 minutes, or until golden brown. Swirl the pan as necessary to distribute the caramel. Stir in the nuts. If any of the sugar crystallizes, continue to cook over low heat to remelt. Pour the nuts and caramel onto a lightly oiled nonstick sheet pan. Let cool and then coarsely chop. Store the praline in an airtight container at room temperature until ready to use.

Olive Oil–Poached Tomatoes

This is a great way to use tomatoes when they are out of season.

YIELD: ABOUT 2 CUPS

6 plum tomatoes

2 cups olive oil

1 sprig fresh rosemary

METHOD—Remove the core from the tomatoes, leaving them whole. Place them standing upright in an ovenproof pan just large enough to hold them. Add the olive oil and rosemary, and cover with aluminum foil. Bake at 275 degrees for 3 to 4 hours, or until the skin easily comes off the tomato. Let cool, remove from the oil, then remove the skins and seeds from the tomatoes. Strain the oil and refrigerate the tomatoes until needed. (The oil will have a pleasant tomato aroma and can be used again.)

*Pear-Caramel Sauce

Try making this sauce with apples or quince.

YIELD: ABOUT 2 CUPS

1 cup sugar

¼ cup orange juice, hot

¼ cup butter

Pulp of 1 vanilla bean

¼ cup heavy cream

10 forelle pears, peeled, cored, and cut into eighths

METHOD—Cook the sugar over medium-low heat for 10 minutes, or until golden brown and caramelized. Add the orange juice and stir until combined. Add the butter, vanilla bean pulp, cream, and pear pieces, and cook for 10 minutes, or until the sauce comes together.

Pickling Juice

The uses are endless, and it keeps indefinitely in the refrigerator.

YIELD: 2 CUPS

1 cup water
½ cup rice vinegar
½ cup plus 2 tablespoons sugar
2 tablespoons kosher salt
1 whole clove
1 teaspoon mustard seed
1 teaspoon black peppercorns
1 teaspoon chopped fresh ginger
½ jalepeño, seeded and chopped

METHOD—Combine all of the ingredients in a saucepan and simmer for 5 minutes, or until the salt and sugar dissolves. Let cool, strain, and use as needed.

Preserved Ginger

You can use the syrup from the ginger for a sauce with a chocolate or apple dessert.

YIELD: ABOUT ¾ CUP

1 cup finely julienned ginger
1½ cups Simple Syrup (see page 215)

METHOD—Blanch the ginger in simmering water for 3 minutes. Strain and repeat the process 2 more times. Simmer the ginger in the simple syrup for 30 minutes. Remove from the heat and cool in the syrup. Refrigerate in the syrup until needed.

Red Wine Jus

This intense reduction can move fish into a red wine course.

YIELD: 1½ CUPS

1½ cups chopped onions
1 cup chopped carrots
1 cup chopped celery
2 tablespoons canola oil
1 Granny Smith apple, chopped
1 orange, peeled and chopped
6 cups Burgundy wine
3 cups port

METHOD—Cook the onions, carrots, and celery in the canola oil in a medium saucepan over high heat for 10 minutes, or until golden brown and caramelized. Add the remaining ingredients and simmer over medium heat for 1 hour. Strain through a fine-mesh sieve and return to the saucepan. Simmer for 30 to 45 minutes, until reduced to 1½ cups.

Roasted Bell Peppers

Purée these peppers with a little olive oil for a great sauce.

YIELD: ABOUT ¾ CUP

4 bell peppers
3 tablespoons olive oil

METHOD—Coat the whole peppers with olive oil. Place on an open grill or flame and roast until black on one side, about 3 minutes. Turn and repeat. Place the roasted peppers in a bowl, cover with plastic wrap, and let stand for 5 minutes. Peel off the skin. Seed, remove the stems, and cut the peppers to the desired size.

213

Roasted Garlic Purée

Always make extra of this. Once you make it, you will find

numerous uses for it.

YIELD: ABOUT ¾ CUP

4 garlic bulbs, tops cut off

3 cups milk

½ cup olive oil

METHOD—Simmer the garlic and milk in a small saucepan for 10 minutes. Drain and discard the milk. Place the garlic bulbs upright in a small ovenproof pan and add the olive oil. Cover with a tight-fitting lid or aluminum foil and bake at 350 degrees for 1½ hours, or until the garlic bulbs are soft.

Cool the garlic in the oil and then squeeze the soft garlic out of the skins. Purée the garlic and the oil until smooth.

Roasted Mushrooms

The juices that come out of the

mushrooms make a great sauce with a

little bit of butter.

YIELD: 1½ CUPS

2½ cups cleaned and stemmed mushrooms

2 sprigs thyme or rosemary

½ cup chopped onion

1 tablespoon olive oil

⅓ cup water

Salt and pepper

METHOD—Place all the ingredients in an ovenproof pan and season to taste with salt and pepper. Cover, and roast at 325 degrees for 30 to 40 minutes, or until tender. Cool in the juices and refrigerate for up to 4 days.

Saffron Tomato Sauce

You can purée this sauce until smooth, or leave it chunky.

YIELD: 1½ CUPS

1 cup julienned red onion

2 tablespoons olive oil

4 cups peeled, seeded, and chopped tomatoes

2 tablespoons balsamic vinegar

¼ cup chopped sundried tomatoes

⅛ teaspoon saffron threads

Salt and pepper

METHOD—Cook the red onions in the olive oil over medium heat for 7 minutes, or until caramelized. Add the tomatoes, balsamic vinegar, sundried tomatoes, and saffron and cook for 20 minutes, stirring occasionally. Remove from heat and purée until smooth. Season to taste with salt and pepper.

Semolina Pasta

You can flavor this pasta with spinach, herbs, or even spices.

YIELD: ABOUT 1½ POUNDS

2 cups extra-fine semolina flour

3 eggs lightly beaten

METHOD—Place the semolina flour and the eggs in a bowl and mix on low speed in an electric mixer fitted with the paddle attachment for 3 minutes, or until the dough comes together. Form the dough into a ball and cover with plastic wrap. Refrigerate for at least 1 hour before using.

Shellfish Oil

This can be made with shrimp or lobster shells, which you can store in the freezer until you have enough.

YIELD: ¾ CUP

4 lobster heads
1 teaspoon tomato paste
1 cup canola oil

METHOD—Roast the lobster heads at 400 degrees for 40 minutes, or until they are bright red in color. Break up the heads and place in a small saucepan with the tomato paste and canola oil. Heat the mixture for 10 minutes, refrigerate for 2 days, and strain through cheesecloth.

Shellfish Stock

This is best when made with the heads of the lobster.

YIELD: 2 QUARTS

5 pounds lobster shells
½ cup chopped carrots
½ cup chopped celery
1 cup chopped leeks
2 tablespoons canola oil
2 tablespoons tomato paste
1 cup red wine

METHOD—Roast the lobster shells in the oven at 400 degrees for 40 minutes or until bright red and slightly golden brown.

Cook the carrots, celery, and leeks in the canola oil over medium-high heat for 10 minutes, or until golden brown and caramelized. Add the tomato paste and cook for 2 to 3 minutes. Deglaze the pan with the red wine and cook for 3 minutes, or until most of the red wine is absorbed. Add the lobster shells and cover three-fourths of the way with cold water. Simmer for 3 hours. Strain through a fine-mesh sieve and simmer for 15 to 20 minutes, or until reduced to 2 quarts.

Simple Syrup

Try adding some citrus zest to this syrup.

YIELD: ABOUT 4 CUPS

2 cups water

2 cups sugar

METHOD—Bring the water and sugar to a boil, remove the pan from the heat, and let cool. The syrup may be kept for up to 1 month in the refrigerator.

Spicy Vinegar

If you like very spicy food, try adding a few habanero chile peppers.

YIELD: 2 CUPS

2 cups assorted whole chile peppers (such as jalapeño or red chiles)

4 sprigs thyme

4 baby carrots, cut in half lengthwise

¼ cup sliced onion

2 cups rice wine vinegar, hot

2 tablespoons olive oil

METHOD—Place the chile peppers, thyme, carrots, onion, and vinegar in a 1-quart container with a lid. Top off with the olive oil and close the lid tightly. Let stand for 2 weeks in the refrigerator, then use as needed.

*Thai Barbeque Sauce

This is great on grilled salmon or duck.

YIELD: ABOUT 3 CUPS

$\frac{1}{2}$ tablespoon sesame oil

1 cup diced Spanish onion

$1\frac{1}{2}$ ounces chopped ginger

1 cup freshly squeezed orange juice

1 teaspoon garlic chili paste

$\frac{1}{4}$ cup honey

5 ounces tomato juice

$\frac{1}{4}$ cup balsamic vinegar

1 cup plum sauce

$\frac{1}{2}$ cup hoisin sauce

$\frac{1}{2}$ cup Worcestershire sauce

$1\frac{1}{2}$ tablespoons Dijon mustard

$\frac{1}{2}$ cup plus 2 tablespoons tamari

1 ounce chopped cilantro

$2\frac{1}{2}$ ounces chopped lemongrass

3 ounces brown sugar

$\frac{1}{2}$ teaspoon paprika

$\frac{1}{2}$ teaspoon salt

$\frac{1}{4}$ teaspoon pepper

METHOD—Heat the sesame oil in a large pan, add the onions, and cook until light brown. Add the ginger and cook for 5 minutes over medium heat. Add the remaining ingredients and cook for 20 minutes. Strain through a fine-mesh sieve and cook for 20 minutes. Let cool and refrigerate until ready to use.

Togarashi

Many Japanese markets carry this all-purpose spice.

YIELD: ABOUT 1¼ CUPS

¼ cup black sesame seeds

¼ cup paprika

2 tablespoons dried basil

2 tablespoons dried bay leaves, ground

2 tablespoons Szechwan black pepper

2 tablespoons cayenne pepper

¼ cup dried red chiles

2 tablespoons sea salt

2 tablespoon orange zest

METHOD—Purée all of the ingredients for 2 minutes, or until finely ground. Store for up to 6 months at room temperature in a tightly sealed container.

Vanilla Simple Syrup

Store old vanilla bean pods in this syrup to give it a more intense flavor.

YIELD: APPROXIMATELY 3 CUPS

2 cups water

2 cups sugar

Pulp and pod of ½ vanilla bean

METHOD—Bring the water, sugar, and vanilla pulp and pod to a boil, remove from the heat, and let cool. The syrup may be kept for up to 1 month in the refrigerator.

Vegetable Stock

The vegetables in this stock can be roasted first for a richer stock.

YIELD: 2 QUARTS

1 cup chopped Spanish onion

1 cup chopped carrot

1 cup chopped celery

1 cup chopped fennel

1 red bell pepper, seeded and chopped

3 cloves garlic

$\frac{1}{2}$ cup chopped parsnip

1 bay leaf

METHOD—Place all of the ingredients in a stockpot and cover with about 4 quarts of cold water. Bring to a boil, reduce the heat to low, and simmer for 1 hour. Strain through a fine-mesh sieve and cook over medium heat for 30 to 45 minutes, or until reduced to 2 quarts.

Wild Mushroom "Consommé"

Once this stock is strained through a coffee filter, it is crystal clear, just like a traditional consommé.

YIELD: 1½ QUARTS

1 pound button mushrooms

2 portobello mushrooms

1 cup shiitake mushrooms

1 cup chopped onion

1 bulb garlic, peeled

3 sprigs fresh thyme

3½ quarts water

METHOD—Combine all of the ingredients in a large stockpot and simmer for 1½ hours. Strain through a coffee-filter-lined sieve.

*These sauces are available at specialty food shops under the *Charlie Trotter's* label. They may also be ordered through Wolferman's by calling 1-800-401-5570, faxing 1-800-401-5534, or through the internet at www.wolfermans.com.

ARUGULA—A slightly bitter, peppery, mustard flavored green that resembles radish leaves. It is great for salads and vegetables dishes.

ASIAN PEAR—A large, round, greenish yellow pear that is quite firm when ripe. They are very juicy with a slightly sweet flavor and a crunchy texture similar to an apple.

BALSAMIC VINEGAR—A dark, sweet, mellow vinegar that is aged in a series of oak and hickory barrels. It is produced only in Modena, Italy, and is used primarily as a dressing. The older the vinegar, the sweeter and less acidic it is. Well-aged balsamic vinegars are available at gourmet food shops.

BASMATI RICE—A long-grain rice from India that has a perfumy, nutlike flavor and aroma.

BEAN THREAD NOODLES—Noodles made from the starch of green mung beans. They are sold dried and must be soaked in hot water before using, unless they are being used in soup.

BELGIAN ENDIVE—A small, slightly bitter cream-colored lettuce that comes in tightly packed cigar-shaped heads.

BLANCHING AND SHOCKING—To briefly plunge a food into boiling salted water and then to immediately place the food into ice water to stop the cooking process. You can use this technique to loosen the skin of fruits such as peaches or tomatoes, or to heighten and set the color and flavor of herbs and greens.

CHIFFONADE—Fine strips about 1/16 inch wide. Usually used in reference to leafy vegetables which are rolled up and finely sliced.

CHORIZO—A spicy, coarsely ground pork sausage widely used in Mexican and Spanish cooking.

CONSOMMÉ—A clarified stock or broth. Traditionally, the stock or broth was clarified by using a combination of egg whites, protein (like ground meat or fish), and acid (such as tomatoes) that form a raft to trap the impurities. But consommés can also be clarified with just the egg white for a lighter flavored consommé.

COQUITOS—Tiny coconuts about the size of a cherry. They are slightly more intense in flavor with a drier flesh than regular coconuts.

CURING—The process of preserving meat or fish. Curing originated before the advent of refrigeration, and was used to hold meat for longer periods of time. These days, curing is more often done for the flavors it provides. Foods can be smoke-cured, as with ham; pickled, as with herring; or salt-cured, as with salt cod.

DAIKON—A large, white Asian radish relatively mild flavored. Excellent for adding texture and just he right amount of bite.

DECANT—To carefully ladle off the liquid substance from a container without disturbing the solids that have fallen to the bottom. This term is commonly used in reference to wine, but also applies to the kitchen when making flavored oils and vinegars.

DEGLAZE—Using a liquid such as wine, water, or stock to dissolve food particles and caramelized drippings left in a pan after roasting or sautéing. The liquid is then used to make a gravy or a sauce.

DERIB—To remove the inner lining of a roasted pepper.

DREDGE—Lightly coating foods with flour, bread crumbs, or cornmeal. Foods are dredged prior to frying to help give them a crispy texture and even, golden-brown color.

EMULSION—A sauce formed when one substance is suspended in another. For example, in hollandaise sauce, melted butter is suspended in partially cooked egg yolks. Emulsions are particularly fragile because they are not a true mixture—if not handled properly they can separate, or break.

FENUGREEK—An herb native to Asia and southern Europe. The seeds can be purchased whole or ground and have a nutty, celery, maple flavor. It is an essential ingredient in curry powder.

FILO DOUGH—Tissue-thin layers of pastry dough used in various Greek and Near East sweet and savory preparations. It is packaged fresh and frozen.

FLAGEOLETS—Tiny, tender, dried French kidney beans that are pale green to creamy white in color.

FRISÉE—A feathery, slightly bitter lettuce with curly yellow-green leaves.

HIJIKI—A dried black seaweed often used to flavor soups and sauces.

HOISIN—A thick, sweet, brownish red sauce made with soy beans, vinegar, sesame seeds, chiles, and garlic. Used in Asian cooking.

INFUSE—To add flavor to a liquid through steeping, as you do when you make tea. The item used to infuse the flavor (usually herbs or spices) doesn't actually stay in the liquid, it just gets left in long enough to impart the flavor and is then removed. Infusing herbs into a hot liquid is a very quick process, sometimes taking only a few seconds. Whereas infusing a flavor into a cold liquid can take several weeks.

JASMINE RICE—A long grain rice from Thailand that has a perfumy, nutty flavor and aroma.

JUICING—The process of extracting the juice from fruits or vegetables. Hand juicers are fine for citrus fruits, but an electric kitchen juicer is most effective for other fruits and vegetables, such as apples, celery, or bell peppers.

KELP—A broad-leafed seaweed, commonly used in Asian cooking for flavoring soups and sauces. Usually sold dried or frozen.

LARDING—Inserting long thin strips of fat or other ingredients into a piece of fish or meat. This cooking technique is performed with a larding needle, which has a sharp tip and a long hollow body into which you insert the strips of fat or other items. The needle is then pulled through the meat, leaving the strips inside.

LEMONGRASS—A scented grass used as an herb in Souteast Asian cooking. Although the whole stalk may be used, usually the outer leaves are removed and only the bottom third of the stalk is used. It has a lemony, strawlike flavor.

MÂCHE—A small-leafed dark green lettuce that has a tangy, nutty flavor.

MARINATE—The process of allowing food to sit in a seasoned liquid. It is sometimes done to tenderize a tough cut of meat, but most often is done to add flavor. Foods that are marinating need to be turned frequently to ensure an even distribution of flavors.

MESCLUN MIX—A mix of salad greens containing arugula, dandelioin greens, frisée, mizuma, oak leaf, mâche, radicchio, and sorrel.

MIRIN—A sweet wine made from glutinous rice. It is available in any Japanese market.

MISO—A fermented soy bean paste used in japanese cooking for making soups, sauces, and dressings. Three types of miso are available at most supermarkets: red, yellow, and white. The three types are very distinct in flavor and should not be substituted for one another.

NORI—Paper-thin sheets of dried seaweed. The color can range from dark green to black. It is generally used for wrapping sushi. When finely cut it serves as a seasoning or garnish.

PANCETTA—A slightly salty Italian bacon that is cured but not smoked.

PAVÉ—The French word for "paving stone," or "cobblestone." In cooking, this term describes any layered preparation cut into a square or rectangle.

PEPITAS—Small green pumpkin seeds that are frequently used in Mexican cooking. They are dark green in color and are sold salted, roasted, or raw.

PONZU—A Japanese sauce with a flavor similar to a rich soy sauce. It is available in most Japanese markets.

QUINOA—A tiny cream-colored, mild-flavored grain. It is often called the 'super grain' because it contains more protein than any other grain. It is also considered a complete protein because it contains all eight essential amino acids.

RADICCHIO—A red-leafed Italian chickory that is most often used as a salad green.

REDUCE—To cook a liquid, such as stocks or broths, until the volume reduces due to evaporation. This process thickens the liquid and intensifies the flavors.

SCORE—The technique of making shallow cuts in the surface of certain foods, such as meat or fish, which allows them to cook evenly.

SOMEN NOODLES—A thin, white Japanese noodle made from wheat flour.

STAR ANISE—A licorice-flavored, star-shaped brown pod containing a seed in each of the star's points.

SUSHI RICE—Also called sticky rice. This short grain rice is very sticky

SWEAT—To cook slowly, uncovered, over medium or low heat with very little fat until soft or translucent.

TABBOULEH—A Middle Eastern dish of bulgar wheat mixed with vegetables and herbs that is usually served cold.

TAMARI SOY SAUCE—A dark soy sauce, somewhat thicker and stronger than other soy sauces. It is cultured and fermented like miso. Used in Asian cooking. In Japanese cuisine it is used as a dipping or basting sauce.

TAMARIND—The fruit of a tall shade tree native to Asia. The large 5-inch long pods contain small seeds and a sour-sweet pulp, which when dried becomes extremely sour.

TEMPER—The process of slowly adding a hot liquid to a cold subtance, while constantly whisking until the cold liquid is warm. This method is often used in making ice cream or custards to prevent the egg yolks from curdling.

TERRINE—Both a terrine mold and the food that has been prepared in the mold. Terrine molds come in many shapes, but they are most commonly rectangular with removable sides (so that the food can be taken out of the mold without damaging the shape of the food). Terrines were traditionally made with pâté or mousses. In modern cooking, however, terrines are usually a combination of layered ingredients.

TOBIKO—Flying fish roe. It comes in orange, red, or wasabi green.

TUILE—A thin, crispy wafer. They are often molded around a curved surface immediately after they come out of the oven , which gives them a shape resembling a curved tile. Tuiles can also be prepared as flat disks and used for layering foods.

WASABI—A pungent, green Japanese horseradish. Available in paste or powder form. The powder. The powder is mixed with water to form a smooth paste.

WATER BATH—The method of placing one container into another water-filled container. A water bath can be used to quickly cool a food product, such as a stock or sauce, by placing the smaller container into ice water held in the larger container. This technique allows the food product to cool without directly touching the water. You can also use a water bath to ensure an even heat distribution when preparing custards and baked puddings—simply bake the custard pan in a larger pan that contains about 1 inch of water.

INDEX

1☉ Ten Speed Press
Box 7123, Berkeley, California 94707
www.tenspeed.com

Distributed in Australia by Simon
& Schuster Australia, Canada by Ten
Speed Press Canada, in New Zealand by
Tandem Press, in South Africa by Real
Books, and in the United Kingdom and
Europe by Airlift Books.

Project coordinator and general editor:
Judi Carle, Charlie Trotter's

Ten Speed Press editor: Lorena Jones

Copyeditor: Suzanne Sherman,
Sebastopol, California

Research, development, and recipe testing:
Sari Zernich, Charlie Trotter's

Graphic design and typesetting:
Three Communication Design, Chicago

Photography: Tim Turner

Illustrations: Matthias Merges and
Mitchell Rice

Library of Congress Cataloging-in-
Publication Data

Trotter, Charlie.
    The kitchen sessions with Charlie
    Trotter/recipes by Charlie Trotter.
    p. cm.
    Includes index.
    ISBN 0-89815-997-0 (alk. paper)
    1. Cookery. 2. Cookery, International.
    I. Title
    TX714.T78 1999
    641.5—dc21

Printed in Singapore by Tien Wah Press
First printing, 1999

4 5 6 7 8 9 10—08 07 06 05 04